SPECIESISM, PAINISM AND HAPPINESS

A MORALITY FOR THE TWENTY-FIRST CENTURY

by

Richard D. Ryder

Foreword by Peter Singer

SOCIETAS
essays in political
& cultural criticism

imprint-academic.com

Copyright © Richard D. Ryder, 2011
The moral rights of the author have been asserted.
No part of this publication may be reproduced in any form
without permission, except for the quotation of brief passages
in criticism and discussion.

Published in the UK by Societas
Imprint Academic, PO Box 200, Exeter EX5 5YX, UK

Published in the USA by Societas
Imprint Academic, Philosophy Documentation Center
PO Box 7147, Charlottesville, VA 22906-7147, USA

ISBN 9781845402358

A CIP catalogue record for this book is available from the
British Library and US Library of Congress

Foreword

by Peter Singer

It is a pleasure to introduce a new philosophical work by Richard Ryder, one of the founders and key figures of the modern animal liberation movement. I first came across Richard's name in 1970, when I was a graduate student in philosophy at the University of Oxford. Through Richard Keshen and then Roslind Godlovitch, I had begun entertaining the thought that our attitudes and practices regarding animals are ethically indefensible. An important part of this new way of thinking about animals was that there is a parallel between the attitudes most of us have towards animals, and the racist and sexist attitudes that almost everyone now rejects. For the attitude to animals that parallels racism and sexism, we had a new word: 'speciesism'. The term came from a leaflet that Roslind showed me. To catch the attention of passers-by, it had a picture of an utterly miserable-looking chimpanzee, who had been infected with syphilis for experimental purposes. But it was the heading - the word 'speciesism' — and the text below the image that made a powerful impression on me. In the text Ryder pointed out that it was selfish of us to think that benefits for our own species justified inflicting misery on other animals. Suffering is, he argued, a clear moral criterion of something bad, and it does not depend on species membership.

This view fitted well within my own broadly utilitarian ethical framework. After all, Jeremy Bentham, the founder of utilitarianism, had written, with regard to animals 'The

Contents

	Foreword by Peter Singer	iv
	Acknowledgements	viii
	Summary	ix
1.	The Quest for Happiness	1
2.	Speciesism	38
3.	Painism	62
4.	Happiness for Others	89
	Glossary	147
	Appendix	148
	Curriculum Vitae	152
	Index	154

question is not, Can they reason? Nor, Can they talk? But, Can they suffer?' (This is now often referred to as Bentham's 'famous footnote' but in 1970, it was not famous at all—it was substantially overlooked in philosophical discussions of Bentham's work.) How could suffering be less morally significant simply because it was the suffering of a being who is not a member of our species?

I got in touch with Richard, who was also living in Oxford and we soon met. That began a long friendship, and a long debate about ethics. We agreed on what I still think is the most critical point, the one on which myself, Ryder, Tom Regan and practically everyone in the animal movement agree: that a difference of species alone cannot provide an ethically defensible basis for giving the interests of one individual more weight than the interests of another. Some twenty years after Richard published his 'Speciesism' leaflet, the philosopher Colin McGinn, writing in *The London Review of Books* described this as 'a won argument'. Most philosophers today, at least in the English-speaking world, would agree with that statement. It is a remarkable transformation of thought, sufficiently radical to be aptly described as a 'revolution'—as Richard did describe it in his chronicle of those changes, intellectual and practical, *Animal Revolution: Changing Attitudes Towards Speciesism*.

Not content with coining the term that sums up what the animal revolution is about, Richard has also played a major role in the practical side of that change, both in reforming the venerable Royal Society for the Prevention of Cruelty to Animals and, perhaps even more significantly, played a leading role, together with the Labour peer Lord Houghton, in making the treatment of animals an issue in electoral politics in the United Kingdom.

Despite our agreement on the issue that divides speciesists from non-speciesists, and our further agreement that pain is a bad thing, Richard and I disagree on a deep ethical issue. What are we to do if the only way to prevent pain to many is to inflict pain on one?

Suppose that the only way to find a cure for a disease that brings suffering and death to millions of humans is to infect a small number of animals with the disease. (This is, of course, a fantasy—in real life experiments on animals can at best offer a small hope of leading, over many years, to a cure for a major disease, and often other methods of research that do not inflict suffering on animals are equally promising.) Repugnant as it would be to inflict on any animal a disease that would cause it to suffer, if there were no other way of finding a cure for the disease without inflicting it on an animal, we would, on my utilitarian view, be justified in doing that experiment, because it would lead to an immense reduction in the number of beings suffering, and in the amount they suffer. This is not a speciesist view, because the experiment could even be justified if the animal in question were a member of the species *Homo Sapiens*. If the member of our species were at the same mental level as a nonhuman animal, and there were no other ethically significant differences, such as the concerns of relatives, then, on a non-speciesist view, there is no reason for thinking it better to use the nonhuman animal than the human.

Richard disagrees, for reasons he explains and defends in this volume. I urge you to read it. I cannot say that I am persuaded by the 'painism' part of his argument, but I do believe that anything Richard writes is worth reading with thoughtful and sympathetic attention.

Princeton University
January 2011

For Barbara

Acknowledgements

I would like to thank Audrey and my children Emily and Henry for encouraging me, Penny Merrett for doing all the real work in the preparation of the manuscript, and Anthony Freeman and Keith Sutherland for being such helpful publishers. I am also grateful to various philosophers with whom I have discussed my ideas over the years and who have helped me to sort them out, including Stephen Law and Julian Baggini and Professors Peter Singer, Tom Regan, Andrew Linzey, Desmond Morris, Harvey Green, John Gray and Anthony Grayling.

Summary

The modern world needs a new morality that is consistent with science and the implications of Darwinism. *Painism* provides such a morality and is based upon the central idea that it is usually wrong to cause suffering to others. All things capable of experiencing suffering should be included within the scope of such a morality. To exclude nonhuman animals is to be guilty of *speciesism* — a prejudice that is no more justifiable than racism or sexism. It is argued that painism should also form the moral basis for government and legislation.

A striking feature of the new theory of *painism* is that it challenges both utilitarianism and democracy by insisting that pains, pleasures and happiness cannot meaningfully be totalled across individuals. So there is no justification for causing pain to one individual for the mere convenience of many. This opens up a range of novel possibilities and, by bridging Utilitarianism and Rights Theory, creates a fresh and unified moral outlook.

CHAPTER 1

The Quest for Happiness

Much of the modern world has no coherent moral policy. There is little exact agreement about what is right and wrong. Moral principles derived from half a dozen great religions conflict and mingle with those drawn from a handful of secular theories. Legislation reflects this confusion and much of Western politics in the twenty-first century, if based upon morality at all, has become a hotchpotch of old religious principles and an odd and incompatible alliance between Utilitarianism and Rights Theory. *There is an urgent need to find a more consistent and unified approach to morals and legislation generally.* This book tries, and I hope not too presumptuously, to provide one possible solution that takes into account the progress of science and the moral implications of Darwinism. This first chapter raises questions about morality and happiness; the last chapter tries to provide some answers.

The popularity of the BBC's radio programme *The Moral Maze* has underlined our fascination with morality as well as the difficulties of the subject. Some of these difficulties arise because we no longer have one moral theory to follow, but many. Contributors to the programme have been deliberately picked so as to reflect differing religious and political positions. Sadly, the BBC has shown itself to be rather old-fashioned on moral matters. For years the moral 'Thought for the Day' on its leading *Today* programme has been given by religious rather than secular speakers and by journalists rather than by ethicists. Over the years it has often been as though the BBC did not realise that Ethics is a well defined academic subject nor been unaware that secular ethical theories, going back to the days of ancient Greece, are formidable additions to the religious positions that their programmes have over-emphasised. *As a first step, we need to accept the idea that morality can exist without god.* Supposed divine approval is, as we shall see, both an unnecessary and an unsatisfactory basis for morality.

Morality remains a challenging subject and there are few easy answers. Some of us have been trying for years to find new solutions to the well established moral conundrums. The old traditional solutions don't quite work. But we all continue to need a straightforward and internally consistent morality, and that is what I am attempting to supply in this volume. In this first chapter I will speculate on the psychology of morality, consider the role of morality in religion, reject relativism, analyse the concept of happiness and its function in morality, classify happiness as a mood, examine the foundations of morality and outline the four current conventional secular moral theories.

So what do we mean by the word 'morality'? It was in the seventeenth century that it was first used to denote a system of morals, where 'moral' refers to the distinction between right and wrong.[1] The word 'ethics' is often taken as being synonymous with 'morality', except that it can also refer to the *study* of morals. There is, however, a further subtle difference between the two words. Whereas 'morality' is derived from the Latin *mores* (meaning 'customs'), 'ethics' is derived from the Greek *ethicos* (meaning 'character'). For this reason *ethics* is sometimes used to describe the theories of Aristotle who focused upon the *character* (i.e. virtues) of moral agents. The term *morality* on the other hand, can be used to concentrate upon *actions*. These two approaches are fundamentally different and underlie many of the disputes within the subject. I shall be focusing upon actions rather than character. Nevertheless I will use the two terms 'morality' and 'ethics' interchangeably.

[1]   The *Shorter Oxford English Dictionary*, OUP, 1933 and 1968

As a devout schoolboy I found myself strapped into an Anglican moral straightjacket that emphasised various quasi-military virtues — discipline, duty, patriotism and physical toughness were among them. It was the overpowering sexual urges of puberty that finally caused me to burst out of these constraints. Why Christianity should be so opposed to sex remains a complete mystery to me. But if it had to be a contest between sex and religion then sex won the day gloriously! Yet, as a confused teenager in the austere 1950s, I continued to think deeply about morality and, roaming alone across the hills of Dorset, I gradually formulated the ideas that are contained in this little book. Much later, I studied what other philosophers had written about ethics. Like many I found myself confused by Aristotle's emphasis upon *virtues*, puzzled by Kant's treatments of *duty*, impressed by the Utilitarians' focus upon *happiness* and liberated by the Rights Theorists' talk of *rights*. But, clearly, all these theories have their faults as well as their good points. Trying to square these four great secular theories with the moral precepts of several religions, and to extract a synthesis that makes sense, seems to have become one of my lifetime hobbies.

I also had to reconcile my interest in ethics with my career as a psychologist. So I frequently found myself thinking about the psychology of morality.

The Psychology of Morality

Why do we need morality? I would suggest that there is both a psychological and a social reason. The psychological derives from our need to be programmed. Our complex and powerful human brains need assistance in making decisions because so many alternative courses of action are open to us. Should we do X or Y or Z? Uncertainty is inherently painful and we feel far happier if we know what we should be doing. So our species' natural longing for morality derives from an internal requirement for certainty in action. Each culture has its own morality but all moralities satisfy this same psychological need for certainty and external guidance. Such guidance is especially welcome when we experience conflicting interests either with others or within ourselves.

As regards the social reason for morality, I believe this is based upon our need to survive in a hostile environment. The human animal has evolved successfully only by working together in families, tribes and nations. On our own we are physically weak. We have needed to cooperate and coordinate our actions with others if we are to succeed. Through the process of natural selection this has meant that those of us who have cooperated have, on average, survived better than those who have been selfish loners. One of the forces that has held humans together cooperatively in this way has been a shared morality—an agreed programme of 'good' actions. So when faced with an external threat, those tribes where members felt a moral duty to act in a unified way and to fight bravely for the common good, survived better than those where people acted only for themselves as individuals.

Two very powerful psychological forces have tended to produce such conformity and cooperation: first, the force of authority, and secondly the force of peer approval. Numerous psychological experiments over the last century have confirmed how effectively the human animal is wired to respond to these two types of external influence. When, for example, we are surrounded by members of our peer group who say that stick A is longer than stick B (when in fact it is slightly shorter) most individuals cave in to peer pressure and agree. Secondly, when instructed by a man in a white coat to give apparently lethal electric shocks to an unwilling human victim, about 60% of ordinary subjects do so. (In fact no shocks were given, and actors were being used in both sets of experiments, but at the time, the subjects did not know this.) Such research by Stanley Milgram and others, demonstrates dramatically that we are predisposed to model our behaviour upon that of our peers and to follow the instructions of those we perceive as being in authority. These are usually the two sources of our moralities. We acquire a day to day morality by copying our peers as regards behaviour that is considered to be good, acceptable or in fashion, and we accept moral instruction from authority figures such as parents, teachers and, ultimately, if we believe in them, from the gods. As a species we are hypersensitive to gaining approval from both these sources. We are innately programmed to conform and to obey. So in moments of painful indecision we look to others and do what we think will meet with their approval. Eventually we 'internalise' the values we believe to be approved and carry them around with us as our conscience or sense of honour. There are, however, some even stronger impulses within us that can drive us to overrule such norms of behaviour, causing us sometimes to break moral conventions and to risk disapproval from both peers and authority figures. Powerful drives such as anger, fear, sex, hunger, parenthood, and the desire for money can force even the most conventional among us to risk disapproval and to do morally unconventional things: a normally honest woman lies to a local council about where she lives so as to enter her children into a better school, a respectable married man suddenly elopes with an attractive young secretary, or a hard-up careerist incurs ruin by accepting a bribe. Among these powerful urges are some that are commonly overlooked, such as disgust, the drive to understand, squeamishness and natural compassion. These may also impinge upon our moral decisions, although some of these basic urges, such as xenophobia, sadism and the drives for power and fame, are still regarded as somewhat shameful in Western culture and so tend not to be easily acknowledged. As a psychologist I like to try to understand human beings by considering us to be drive-machines, pushed in various directions by such drives. The *potential* for these drives is born into us although their detailed forms are fashioned, to an extent, by the environments in which we live.

Is morality itself a drive? In some senses I suspect that it is. Typically, for a drive, it is an innate core tendency that is directed and moulded by learning. So do any of the other animal species on our planet show any signs of morality? The answer is that they almost certainly do. Look at the guilty expression of a pet dog found raiding the larder. That dog has certainly learned what is right and wrong! Recent research has found that many species show empathy not only for their own kind but even for individuals of other species. Dolphins have protected humans from shark attacks. Chimpanzees will refuse food to prevent injury to their peers. Elephants mourn their dead. Human infants show the gradual appearance of empathy and by early childhood, so I believe, can show four spontaneous types of concern for others that eventually form the building blocks of morality:

- A sense of justice or fairness
- Affection for parents, pets and toys
- Empathy for the sufferings of others (including animals)
- A desire for freedom

Research has found that when babies as young as three months hear crying, they cry, and when infants see suffering in others they will try to help.[2]

When we are older, these impulses naturally develop into strong protective feelings for siblings, mates and offspring, affectionate feelings that manifest as grooming, stroking, feeding and caring, as well as general cooperation and support for 'the herd'. Gradually such impulses become generalised and intellectualised and take on a moral character. Brain scans have suggested that both 'emotional' and 'rational' parts of the brain are implicated in ethical decision-making generally. This may confirm the notion that what becomes morality are basic drives that are moulded by learning.

Is there a Physical Basis for Morality?

Being religious and believing in God are now known to be behaviours that are partly genetically determined; such behaviours run in families, and identical twins correlate on religiousness significantly more than do non-identical twins. Hungering after a morality is probably in a similar

---

[2] Paul Bloom: That Warm Fuzzy Feeling, *New Scientist*, 16 October 2010

category — as common as the hunger for religion but somewhat independent from it. This independence allows for many people to feel strongly the need for a moral code without feeling any similar compulsion to be religious or to connect the two.

It has long been known to psychologists that damage to the frontal lobes of the brain can lead to impairments in moral behaviour. A previously virtuous person, with frontal damage may become aggressive, slovenly, unreliable, impulsive, self-centred, lacking in foresight and disinhibited sexually. In normal people altruistic behaviour can depend either upon the cool and reasoned application of a moral theory or upon the spontaneous flow of compassionate feelings, or both. The former will involve processing by the cerebral cortex (including the frontal lobes) whereas the latter will also include sub-cortical emotional structures. Studies of the neurophysiological basis for empathy and compassion are progressing but not yet conclusive. Moral judgements have been shown to be affected by magnetic impulses to the skull near the right temporal parietal junction, which apparently reduce levels of empathy. Increased levels of the neuropeptides vasopressin and oxytocin, on the other hand, lead to increased levels of empathy and attachment. Increased serotonin, too, not only reduces depression but increases aversion to harming others. Antidepressant drugs that increase serotonin also have this effect, and this is especially true in individuals who already show high levels of trait empathy. Scans indicate that moral judgements tend to involve hypothalamus, amygdala, and anterior cingulate cortex as well as the ventro-medical prefrontal cortex. Furthermore, changes in the right amygdala and the anterior cingulate cortex are associated with empathetic behaviour.[3] *Ultimately, moral behaviour will be exactly correlated with brain physiology and with the action of certain brain systems.* Recent brain scan research suggests that any state of belief itself (whether religious or non-religious), is associated with the same areas of the brain (principally the ventromedial prefrontal cortex).

[3]   M J Crockett et al, *Proc. Nat. Acad. Sci* 107(40), 2010

Religious statements and non-religious statements, on the other hand, are processed in separate areas, the former being more associated with emotional systems and the latter with memory.[4]

Children show natural tendencies to try to make sense of the world, to best remember stories with exciting magical content, to be influenced by absent or fantasy figures, to fear supernatural punishment for wrongdoing and to tend to attribute deliberate purpose or intention to natural events. These all encourage religious and superstitious tendencies. We grow up, after all, in a world we do not entirely understand. Even today, with our advanced scientific knowledge, much that happens to us (accidents, illnesses, wins on the lottery etc.) have unknown causes and so can easily be attributed to 'luck', 'fate', or 'chance'. Quantum mechanics, the cutting edge of modern science, has itself encouraged this tendency with its emphasis upon probability and indeterminability rather than upon clearly determined causes. Events are no longer seen as occurring inevitably according to hard Newtonian rules, but in a far less predictable fashion according to random influences, whether or not they are observed, or by 'decisions' apparently made by the sub-atomic particles themselves. So, between the so-called laws of physics there are now perceived to be huge spaces where luck, fate and chance can easily be believed to play a powerful role. Paradoxically, we still tend to believe in our own powers to determine events. Maybe it is because we believe in our own 'free will' that we tend to believe that natural events are being similarly willed. As children we experience the effects of our own will: we throw a stone and a window breaks, we kiss our mother and she smiles, or we hit our sister and she cries. So we naturally tend to conclude that many other important events must, similarly, be the results of an unseen will or sense of purpose. Free-will we will return to later as it is one of the most vexed of all moral issues. (See Chapter 3, Painism) Almost certainly it does not

---

[4] S. Harris, J.T. Kaplan, A. Curiel, S.Y. Bookheimer, M. Iacoboni et al., The Neural Correlates of Religious and Non Religious Belief, *PLoS ONE* 4(10), 2009

exist, except as an illusion: or is it, too, saved by modern quantum theory?

Morality as a Central Component in Religion

Perhaps the most important part of all religions is the teaching of morality. There is not any religion that does not lay down or imply a code of 'good' behaviour. Indeed, there is a remarkable degree of agreement among the major religions on what is to be considered right and wrong. Telling the truth, keeping promises, protecting members of the family, not stealing, cheating or murdering, are examples of common, indeed almost universal, moral precepts. In the religions these precepts are often founded upon the claim that they are the will of God — the ultimate figure of authority. The overarching moral principle behind all these precepts, however, is the Golden Rule: *do not do to others what you would not like to be done to you*. This 'do as you would be done by' principle underlies Confucianism, Judaism, Islam, Buddhism, Jainism, Taoism and Christianity.[5] All these religions respect this Golden Rule although sometimes forgetting it in practice.

All religions satisfy the same psychological needs and, as we have seen, the need for moral certainty is one of the most important. But there are other psychological benefits of religion such as the calming reassurance gained from the repetition of dogma and ritual, and from the often offered prospect of eternal life. The claim by religions to *explain* the universe (its creation, purpose and how it works) and the claim that prayer and ritual have the power to *control* the course of events (for example, to grow crops, defeat enemies and cure illness) also stand out. I have elsewhere described these three great psychological functions of religion as providing:

- moral certainty
- an explanation for the universe
- an alleged power to control events

---

[5] Karen Armstrong: *The Great Transformation*, Atlantic Books, London, 2006

I have called these the mechanisms of *morality, meaning and magic*, respectively, and pointed out that the last two are now supplied by science. Modern science provides far more convincing descriptions of how the universe works and supplies overwhelmingly more powerful and reliable technological 'magic' with which to control events. What science has not provided, however, is a morality.

Disbelief in god is now a widespread condition. Perhaps half the human species does not strongly believe in any god whereas nearly everyone believes in science because everywhere they can see its achievements—in medicine, atomic power, electricity, the internet, television, radio, aviation, agriculture, modern weaponry and space travel. There seems little evidence for the existence of a powerful god, especially not a benign one, but the evidence of the effectiveness of science is everywhere about us. Are those of us without a god to have no morality? No, what is clearly needed now is a morality that does not depend upon any fixed idea of god but is clearly and rationally argued and supported, where it needs to be, by the findings of science itself. To have no agreed morality could mean a chaotic end to human society.

The founders of the great religions often come across as compassionate figures, however irrational or mistaken. Jesus, for example, had emphasised two moral principles above all others. The first was to 'love the Lord your God' while the second was to 'love your neighbour as yourself' (Mark 12.29–31). It was a moral position already emphasised in the Jewish tradition by Hillel—a great teacher during Jesus' boyhood. But Jesus went on to urge his followers to also 'love your enemies' (Luke 7. 27) and this was a fairly new moral precept. Furthermore, Jesus always supported the underdog—'blessed are the meek' he said, (Matthew 5. 5) and the 'persecuted'. He also said—'Do to others as you would have them do to you' (Luke 7.31), and here we return to the Golden Rule. One of the most interesting aspects of the Golden Rule is that its basis is not in the alleged word of God but in our own feelings about others. So, to an extent, this is a step taken by Hillel and

The Quest for Happiness

Jesus to humanise the basis of morality. It no longer depends entirely upon divine will but upon applied empathy, common suffering and compassion. There are within all of us these two great conflicting instincts of selfishness and compassion, and it is the rationalisation, reinforcement and application of the latter that form the basis for many moralities including my own. (The less attractive aspects of Jesus' moral attitudes — his possible callousness towards mental illness, animals, the divorced, the environment, witches and unbelievers — we have no need to dwell upon here.)

Relativism

Relativism — which has plagued the discussion of ethics in the late twentieth century — has argued that moral values are merely culturally determined and that everyone should be allowed to follow their own culture. So, if you have been brought up to believe that tearing the heart out of living humans as a sacrifice is a worthy thing to do, then you should be entitled to continue with this practice. Similarly, you may believe that it is good to cut out the clitoris of young girls, to hang witches or to burn reluctant widows. Relativism claims that if such values are part of your culture then you should be permitted to carry on regardless of the screams of your victims.

Clearly there has to be something seriously wrong with this argument. It is as if the Allies had no moral justification for trying to overthrow the Nazis in the Second World War. At the Nuremberg trials, did the Allies argue that if the Nazis sincerely believed it was a good thing to kill innocent Jews then it was their cultural right to do this? Did the Allies say to Hitler: 'I can believe one thing and you can believe the opposite and both are true *for us*'? No! The objection to such sophistry is that the *victims' consents had not been given*. These are powerful examples of where the consideration of the innocent victims' wishes should be of far greater importance than focusing on the character of the moral agent. I dare say many Aztec priests, East African cultists, Hindu traditionalists, English witchfinders and even Nazis were perfectly sincere and dutiful people when they did what they did. Some may have shown traditional Aristotelian moral virtues such as courage, skill, intelligence, patience, temperance and even (by their own lights) justice! They might also conceivably have shown Kantian 'good intention'. But what they did not show was compassion towards their victims. Did their victims give their informed and absolutely free and well-considered consent to have their heart or clitoris cut out, or to be burned, hanged or gassed? No, they did not!

We can accept that all human societies need moral standards. Does it matter that some societies' standards are dramatically opposed to those of other societies? Can we just say to ourselves when faced by widow-burning, vivisection or genital mutilation: 'Well if that's the way they do it, it's alright by me — it's none of my business'? Are we not allowed to say that some moral standards are universal? That such things are wrong wherever or whenever they occur? I believe we are.

Happiness as the Aim of Morality

What, then, is the aim of morality? What is the yardstick for deciding whether an action is a good or a bad thing? Well, in the absence of any supernatural or religious criteria, we have to answer these questions in a more down-to-earth manner. Surely, in a fundamental sense, *whatever makes me happy or gives me pleasure* is, prima facie, good. But only for me. For others it may not be a good thing. A man who eats all the available food on a desert island may have done good for himself but not for the other islanders. Sharing the food or giving it all to others are behaviours that might well be considered morally good, whereas eating it all myself may be good for me in survival terms, but is almost certainly wrong morally. So a very great deal depends upon the identity or locus of the beneficiary of an action — on who benefits from it.

This is why I believe that morality can only be about how I treat others. What I like to do for myself is a matter for *psychology* to consider, while doing for others what *they* like is the essence of *morality*. What is it then that they like? Clearly, they like pleasures rather than pains, and they like the general and prolonged state of being happy. It may sound a bit obvious to say that the essence of morality is about making others happy but it is surely true. The strange thing is how seldom it is said, as if 'happiness' is a dirty word. Indeed, until the late twentieth century the word was avoided by serious writers. Yet psychologists have found repeatedly that when people are asked what they want or seek to attain in life, the final answer is always the same — happiness. For example, the initial answer to the question 'what do you want from life?' may be 'money', 'fame', 'love' or 'success'. But if these replies are followed up repeatedly by further probes as to why they want money, fame, love or success the respondent will eventually end up answering that it is because he believes money, fame, love or success will make him happy. But when asked why he wants happiness he will react with amazement — well it's obvious, everyone wants happiness! No further explanation is considered necessary or possible. More lofty-sounding aims such as liberty, justice, equality and fraternity are found to have the same origins. When asked why he seeks such conditions a respondent will ultimately agree it is because he believes liberty, justice, equality or fraternity will increase his or others' happiness. So it is with all other ideals. They are all perceived to be means to obtaining happiness. Of course, 'happiness' is a difficult word to define, but so are many others. This is not an excuse for not trying to do so.

Overall, one can say that happiness tends to be increased by pleasures and by the reduction of pains of any sort. This should hardly come as a surprise to any psychologist and particularly not to any old-fashioned behaviourist who (rightly) saw learned behaviour as the consequence of negative reinforcement (pain) or positive reward (pleasure, including the avoidance or reduction of pains). Jeremy Bentham, the father of Utilitarianism, understood all this and built his moral theory upon it. He was right to do so. It may seem obvious that we all seek happiness but some moralists carry on as if this was in doubt. Just as the ultimate *psychological* objective of each individual is his or her happiness, so the ultimate *moral* objective should be the happiness of *other* individuals. Clearly, we need to explore this all important thing called happiness.

So-called Positive Psychology has considered the issue but its initial findings have not met with widespread acclaim. This school has attracted considerable amounts of attention but has so far failed to discover techniques for producing long-lasting happiness[6] or even for measuring it. The only convincing measure of happiness is self-reported happiness, in reply to simple questions such as 'how happy are you?' or 'are you happy?' Answers to such questions are known to be unreliable over time. Self-reported measures of happiness can too easily become measures of *hopefulness*. Yet they are the best we have. Indeed, as happiness is a subjective experience, it makes no sense to look for objective measures for it until valid physiological correlates are established.

On average people say they are no happier today than they were fifty years ago when incomes were half what they are today.[7] Clearly, affluence and material improvements are not so crucial for human wellbeing as economists once assumed. Happiness, as it is experienced, is not exactly a perception nor an idea nor even an emotion. So what is it? We need to find a new descriptive category for happiness. I will conclude that happiness is usually what we call a mood. (See pp 23–29)

Some Traditional Views of Happiness

Aristotle, who emphasized the importance of happiness, suggested two forms:

- *hedonia* (pleasure), and
- *eudaimonia* (contentment)

---

[6] Aaron Jarden and Dan Weijers: Wipe that Smile off your Face, *The Philosopher's Magazine*, 1st quarter 2011, pp. 53–59

[7] Layard, Richard: *Happiness : Lessons from a New Science*, Penguin Books, London, 2006

In literature, happiness is traditionally associated with four things — good luck, love, success and prosperity. These suggest elements of chance, romance, fulfilled ambition and material sufficiency respectively. Desmond Morris has pointed out that happiness also has a literary reputation for being elusive, unpursuable and varied.[8] Some writers claim that it arises from a sense of lifetime achievement, some that it is found in trivia, some that it comes from triumph over others. A more charitable view is that happiness can only be found in cooperation, in the rational and intellectual life, or in a clear conscience. More cynically, others have connected happiness with stupidity, irrationality or escapist fantasy. For Samuel Johnson happiness consists in 'the multiplicity of agreeable consciousness' and can be found either in 'wisdom' or 'a good tavern'. For Ibsen happiness thrives in 'life-lies', for Dryden in 'rest from pain', for Horace in 'boats and carriage rides', for Kant not in an 'ideal of reason but of imagination'. For Pope happiness is 'our being's end and aim'. For Gray happiness 'too swiftly flies', while Shaw claims to believe that a lifetime of happiness would be 'hell on earth' and that 'we have no right to consume happiness without producing it'. For Jefferson the pursuit of happiness is 'a right', for Jane Austen 'a large income is the best recipe for happiness', for F H Bradby 'the secret of happiness is to admire without desiring', for Fanny Burney 'travelling is the ruin of all happiness', for Maria Edgeworth's young ladies — 'a love match was the only thing for happiness', while Aldous Huxley's philosophers gained happiness by watching Autumn's sunsets or in 'eyeing the gorgeous buttocks of the ape'. Perhaps more persuasively there have been claims that happiness is to be found 'in tranquility of mind' (Cicero), as 'an enemy to pomp and noise' (Joseph Addison) or in 'accepting change gracefully' (James Stewart). It is clearly all very complicated. As Richard Whately once remarked — 'happiness is no laughing matter'.

Aristotle used the word 'eudaimonia' to describe what can best be called *contentment*, and that seems to be a com-

---

[8] Desmond Morris, *The Nature of Happiness*, Little Books, London, 2006

mon view of the state of happiness itself, while its proposed ingredients can mostly be described as pleasures.

A debate on the question of happiness was orchestrated by Denise Inge at Dartington in 2010.[9] Some forty 'lay' participants, including myself, raised many different issues on the subject. Groucho Marx's opinion that 'I, not events, have the power to make me happy or unhappy' received almost universal support until a depressive in the group said that, when depressed, her unhappiness was way beyond her control. Several people stressed the need for 'a balance of joy and sorrow' or 'a balance between having company and being alone' as being the secret to a happy life. This rather pessimistic faction thought that 'lack and longing' always persist even in happiness and that 'this shadow gives depth' to our lives. Others considered that unhappiness is a more definite state than is happiness. Guilt, fear and insecurity can all intensify unhappiness, as can almost any kind of loss. On the other hand 'a meaning in life' was perceived as a source of happiness, supporting Helen Keller's view that happiness is not attained through self-gratification, but 'through fidelity to a worthy purpose'. People also favoured Samuel Johnson's opinion that 'hope is itself a species of happiness and, perhaps, the chief happiness which this world affords'. So it seems that hopes for the future, just as happy memories of the past, can all enhance happiness in the present. Security was seen as a source of felicity too—even a 'humdrum routine' could be valuable according to the pessimists. 'Value what you've got' was a repeated theme. No definitive answers were reached as to which ingredients of happiness are necessary and which are sufficient. The troubled relationship between pains, pleasures and happiness, raised by Bentham's and Mill's theories, was not settled. No actual definition of happiness was agreed, nor distinctions (if there are any) established between happiness, contentment, bliss, ecstasy, serenity, joy, fulfilment, euphoria or mania. There was, by the end of the debate, just a hint that some participants were realising

---

[9] Denise Inge: Debate on *Searching for Happiness* at *Ways with Words*, Dartington, 17 July 2010. Printed with Permission

the importance of mood and its underlying neuro-chemistry. Not only the depressive but others were pointing out that 'some people are definitely born unhappy or happy' and that exercise can cause happiness through the release of 'adrenaline or endogenous opiates'.

A debate chaired by Peter Stanford at Lippiano in Italy later in the same year came up with a similar conclusion. A consensus was reached among the twenty participants that some people are 'born to be happy' and some are not. Such cheerful types show a stoic jollity in the face of life's troubles. Is this due to certain learned attitudes and mind-sets, or is it once again a matter of intrinsic biochemistry or mood? The meeting could not quite make up its mind on this.

Some Personal Views on Happiness, Pleasure and Pain

To me there seem to be three main causes of pleasure and all three can also enhance happiness:

- the satisfaction of our drives (such as hunger, sex, ambition, companionship, parenthood etc.)
- the relief of psychological and so-called 'physical' pains (ranging from stomach aches to such states as anxiety, insecurity, grief, fear, guilt and lack of self-esteem);
- the experience of *direct pleasures* such as warmth, music, beautiful sights and smells.

It can be argued that the first two (the satisfaction of drives and the relief of pain) are virtually the same because any unsatisfied drive state is itself painful.

We clearly need to get away from the idea that pleasures are only to do with the senses. The taste of good food, comforting massage, sexual ecstacy or a beautiful perfume are not the end of the story at all. Such *sensory* pleasures are just the beginning. Pleasures can also be *emotional* (loving, being loved, experiencing joy, gratitude, friendship, reunion, pride), *aesthetic* (the pleasure in beauty) and *cognitive* pleasures (e.g. of imagination, intellectual achievement, understanding and mental exploration). Pains fall into similar categories of being either *sensory* (the so-called 'physical' pains), *emotional* (e.g. grief, anxiety, fear, guilt, shame, disgust) or *cognitive* (e.g. pain derived from intellectual frustration or conflict, as well as from the failure to understand). Is there an aesthetic equivalent of pain? Extremes of ugliness, dirt, deformity, lack of order and the perception of injury and disease can produce very strong negative reactions indeed, but I would regard these all as *emotional* pains. How far does the aesthetic category really stand separate from the emotional at all? A bad smell can be so repulsive that it produces vomiting or fainting. So stench is surely a cause of pain. But is it aesthetic, emotional or merely sensory? Initially it is sensory but its negative effects can clearly spread far wider; as can the effects of painfully perceiving the injury, suffering or death of others. So when I am talking of pains or pleasures I am talking about a huge range of experiences. Arguably, every experience (sensory, emotional or cognitive) we label as either painful or pleasurable. There may be no such thing as a neutral experience that is neither pleasurable nor painful.

Evidence suggests that mood profoundly affects these experiences so that if we are in a happy mood our experiences tend to be more pleasurable, whereas if we are depressed we find it hard to enjoy anything. However slight, every experience probably carries an algesic value, either pleasurable or painful. It seems that all the usual concepts in ethics are also strongly charged in this way. Principles such as liberty, equality, justice and fraternity are all valued positively because they are believed to be potent sources of pleasure (which they usually are), whereas the lack of them are considered potent sources of pain. Autonomy, justice, truthfulness are further examples. Even virtues such as magnanimity, courage, patience and humility can be seen as traits that tend to lead to pleasure in others, whereas vices such as greed, anger and envy tend to produce pain for others. Above all, duties and rights all seem, ultimately, aimed at reducing pains and increasing pleasures. This is why I believe that ethics is ultimately about pain and pleasure, about what others like and dislike, about their welfare and their suffering. Pains and pleasures are important because they are the obvious components of happiness, and happiness is what we should be seeking to produce in others.

Pains, of course, usually have a strongly negative effect upon happiness. Happiness is very sensitive to pain. Pain can easily disrupt contentment. Bliss and toothache do not mix. Any pain, sensory, cognitive or emotional, can be like a drop of ink in a glass of clear water — within seconds the water is tainted. Research is beginning to confirm this and to demonstrate that a pain is far more powerful than is a pleasure. Pain tends to dominate. Of course, pain is a complex issue psychologically and it can be ignored, denied and almost totally rendered unconscious by the force of suggestion. In hypnosis, for example, the awareness of pain can be made to vanish. On the other hand, some people, perhaps the more thoughtful, tend to be pain sensitizers. They cannot ignore a pain and tend to focus their attention upon it. Those who can push a pain out of their mind tend to do better. Masochists even appear to enjoy pain but that is only because they derive a pleasure from the pain that is even greater than the pain. (This may be because the pain cancels out the guilt associated with a particular pleasure, or because a particular pleasure has been previously associated with pain so that the pain 'triggers' or enhances the pleasure.) Within all of us there is this constant pain-pleasure balancing act. We have an internal mechanism that balances all our current pains against all our current pleasures. At any one moment there is a net balance — either positive or negative. I would hesitate to equate happiness with a positive balance of pleasures over pains but it is probably almost the same thing. At any one time I may be experiencing a score of pains and a hundred minor pleasures. I may, for example, be feeling a slight headache, a feeling of guilt for not having written a thank-you letter to my aunt, a dislike of the smell of yesterday's lunch, and a nagging worry that I am not going to see my girlfriend until Wednesday. Perhaps this adds up to 50 units of pain as a total. Against this my brain balances the total of current good feelings such as my recent enjoyment of a cup of mint tea, a pleasant memory that England has won the Test Match, some enjoyable thoughts about Immanuel Kant, a sense of relief that my backache has disappeared, and a pleasant expectation that I am going to have lunch with Barbara. If all these pleasures add up to only 40 units then I may, overall, feel a bit miserable because this total is less than my total of current pains. If, on the other hand, they add up to over 50 then I will feel happy!

It should perhaps be noted that wherever clinical depression is precipitated by environmental events these usually *take the form of loss*: loss of loved ones, loss of purpose, loss of job, loss of home, loss of respect, loss of love, loss of money or precious possessions. To avoid such disappointments in life Buddha and others have counselled that it is wise to avoid attachment to such things. This is easier said than done for most of us. Would it produce a better result anyway? A society filled by isolated and selfish gurus, neglectful parents, heartless lovers and weird loners? The corollary, however, is interesting: that *the antidote for reactive depression should be acquisition*: the acquiring of lovers, friends, approval, status, art, food, clothes, pets or money. Gain is good and an anti-depressive. As a form of self-therapy, acquisition or gain is extremely common — so-called 'retail therapy' and even compulsive shop-lifting being cases in point. Many people, feeling threatened by incipient unhappiness, simply go out shopping! Perhaps society could put acquisition upon a more organised basis. Of course, such solutions to unhappiness usually have only a temporary effect, but then life itself is only temporary!

A Traditional Route to Happiness?

So how do we find happiness? There are some who argue that a return to Old Testament values is the answer. Ann Widdecombe, for example, has proposed that the route to happiness is by following the Ten Commandments and through the suppression of those natural impulses condemned by them.[10] Let us have a look at these foundations of Western morality. I quote them verbatim:

- I am the LORD your God, who brought you out of Egypt, out of the land of slavery. You shall have no other gods before me.

- You shall not make for yourself an idol in the form of anything in heaven above or on the earth beneath or in the waters below. You shall not bow down to them or worship them; for I, the LORD your God, am a jealous God, punishing the children for the sin of the fathers to the third and fourth generation of those who hate me, but showing love to a thousand generations of those who love me and keep my commandments.

- You shall not misuse the name of the LORD your God, for the LORD will not hold anyone guiltless who misuses his name.

- Observe the Sabbath day by keeping it holy, as the LORD your God has commanded you. Six days you shall labour and do all your work, but the seventh day is a Sabbath to the LORD your God. On it you shall not do any work, neither you, nor your son or daughter, nor your manservant or maidservant, nor your ox, your donkey or any of your animals, nor the alien within your gates, so that your manservant and maidservant may rest, as you do. Remember that you were slaves in Egypt and that the LORD your God brought you out of there with a mighty hand and an outstretched arm. Therefore the LORD your God has commanded you to observe the Sabbath day.

- Honour your father and your mother, as the LORD your God has commanded you, so that you may live long and that it may go well with you in the land the LORD your God is giving you.

- You shall not murder.

- You shall not commit adultery.

- You shall not steal.

---

[10] Ann Widdecombe, *The Bible: A History*, Channel 4 Television, 7 February 2010. The Ten Commandements are quoted here from Deuteronomy 5.6–22; cf. Exodus 20.1–17.

- You shall not give false testimony against your neighbour.
- You shall not covet your neighbour's wife. You shall not set your desire on your neighbour's house or land, his manservant or maidservant, his ox or donkey, or anything that belongs to your neighbour.

These are the commandments the LORD proclaimed in a loud voice to your whole assembly there on the mountain from out of the fire, the cloud and the deep darkness; and he added nothing more. Then he wrote them on two stone tablets and gave them to me.

Moses was, no doubt, trying to do his best to control the tough Bronze Age tribal society he led. He needed the social cohesion that would be facilitated by a shared system of morals and, in order to get these rules accepted by a superstitious people, he invested them with divine authority. He based his system, to an extent, upon contemporary Egyptian principles.

Few in modern times would argue strongly against the Ten Commandments' moral disapproval of murder, false witness, covetousness or theft, nor would they strongly quibble over the honouring of parents (despite some parents being awful), although more might question the alleged importance of observing the Sabbath, and the relevance today of not worshipping idols or misusing the name of God. To the modern mind these things appear to be trivial. On occasions, the restraints over our sexual, violent and envious impulses, as ordered in the Ten Commandments, may well enhance the happiness of others, although not necessarily our own happiness. Adultery, then regarded almost as a form of theft, is today seen as a more complex issue. It is, incidentally, the only form of sexual behaviour which is mentioned in the Ten Commandments. In general, of course, the *expression* of our impulses rather than their *restraint* has been accepted by psychologists as a far more likely route to personal happiness for those who express them; frustration all too often causes anger and distress. Like many early moral tracts the Ten Commandments are very ambiguous as to whose happiness (if any) they seek to promote; the doer's, the victim's or God's.

The seven deadly sins were invented over a thousand years later as a guide to Christian morality. They are pride, envy, greed, gluttony, sloth, lust and anger, as listed by Pope Gregory the Great (and not the Bible). Again, there is confusion as to why they are considered sins. Do they allegedly damage god or the person who experiences them, or others? In fact, the first three are all narcissistic and rather interrelated. Gluttony is certainly bad for our health. Sloth, too, is unhealthy and may well be a sign of depression. If lust means an *excessive* preoccupation with sexual desire then it may indicate wider problems. Anger, although just as natural as lust is a common source of violence. Nevertheless, anger at the perception of cruelty or injustice to others, often provides the motivation for reform. This list does not seem to have been well 'thought through' by Gregory!

Can Happiness be Re-Classified as Mood?

There has been some talk in recent years about adding to the list of the experiences we usually call emotions (or feelings). The classic four emotions are fear, grief, joy and anger. To this it has been proposed to add at least disgust and surprise. But there are many other states that could be included such as shame, guilt, pride, passion, affection, envy, greed, pity, jealousy and even lust. Whether or not anything is to be gained from giving such states the label of 'emotion' is debatable. Today's psychologist would usually agree that most emotions have probable advantages in terms of evolutionary survival. These are the emotions that also have a 'drive' component which pushes us to behave in a certain way. Fear prompts flight and anger encourages fight, for example. Affection is linked to the care of children, spouses and kin, while lust drives procreation, and even envy and jealousy can push us towards general self-improvement. Disgust and squeamishness help us to avoid disease and danger. It is interesting, however, that two groups of emotions do not have obvious survival functions. Most basically these are positive emotions like joy and negative ones like grief. It happens to be these emotions, too, that are most closely linked with happiness, either in a positive or a negative way.

They are, as I have proposed, also associated with what psychiatrists and clinical psychologists have long called 'mood'. Mood has been defined as 'a relatively pervasive and sustained emotional state'.[11] At one extreme, mood is associated with clinical depression and melancholy, at the other with high spirits and mania. Moods characteristically colour perceptions and thoughts. There are at least four types of mood, in my opinion, and these are like prolonged versions of the four classic emotions of grief, joy, anger and fear. They are pervasive and endure for more than a few moments. All in all, *I would like to describe happiness itself as a mood.*

Depression is an extremely common mood disorder while mania (characterised by euphoria, over-activity, pressure of speech, flight of ideas and disinhibition) is much rarer, and those who fluctuate from one extreme mood to another are labelled as being manic-depressive or bipolar. (The lifetime risk of serious bipolar disorder is 0.6 - 1.1% in the adult US population.) Some moods, however, can be changed by events. Bereavement or other loss is the frequent precipitant of depression whereas triumph, achievement, reunion or acquisition can promote a happy mood. But, strangely perhaps, some moods appear to be independent of events and it is these so-called 'endogenous' mood states that can result in the most severe symptoms. Paradoxically, it is also these conditions of severe depression or mania that can best respond to medication. Mania, in addition to raised levels of dopamine and serotonin, is correlated with raised nor-adrenaline.

---

[11] Arthur Reber and Emily Reber: *Dictionary of Psychology*, Penguin Books, 1985

Mood: the Innate Factor

All of us tend to have our own average levels of mood and characteristic patterns of mood-change. Some of us tend most of the time to be rather low in spirits, taciturn or pessimistic, while others are irrepressibly jolly and active. Nearly all the successful self-made people I have met have been in this latter camp although some of them also suffer sharp but short depressions. Almost every combination of moods is possible. There are those of us who are steadily a little high or low and who never show much change. There are also those who keep an even keel in the middle — neither particularly high nor low. Most of us, however, change a little, one way or the other, so we know that if we are a bit low one day we will not find pleasures quite so enjoyable as usual and if we are a bit high the next we will enjoy all sorts of things that leave others quite cold. Such experiences seem to me to be highly pertinent to the mystery of happiness. When asked if he is happy the severe depressive, even though he may have wealth, fame, a loving family and physical health, will say that he is still miserable. On the other hand, someone who is in an elevated mood state, even though he may be out of work, bereaved and impecunious, will nevertheless still maintain that he is happy. Whatever tends to elevate our mood-state a little but not too much, whether it is external circumstances or some spontaneous internally prompted swing is, I believe, the key to happiness. Mild stimulants, opioids and drugs such as ecstasy and cannabis can all induce euphoria, although there are sometimes undesirable side-effects. Traditional morality may be offended to consider such means to happiness as legitimate, and sometimes on good grounds such as the risk of addiction, violence, damage to health or judgement. Such euphoria-inducing drugs are, admittedly, short-cuts. But in the future it seems highly likely that euphoriants which lack side-effects may become freely available. Under these circumstances traditional moralists may find that they lack rational grounds for disapproval. The notion that it is 'not natural' to seek happiness with drugs will begin to sound insufficient. At that juncture society may divide between a

TABLE ONE

The Causes of Happiness

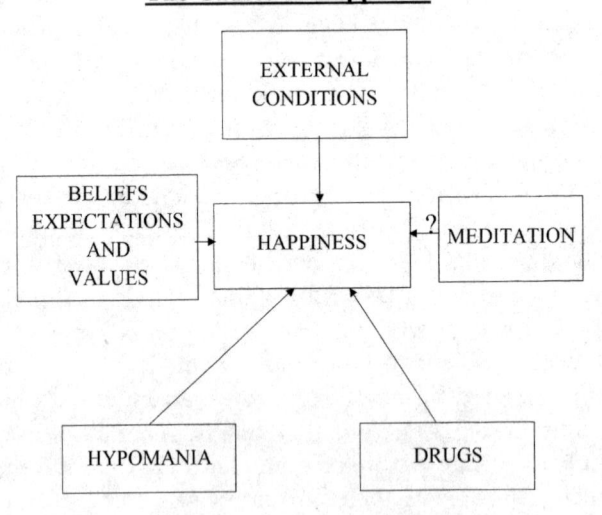

```
                    ┌──────────────┐
                    │   EXTERNAL   │
                    │  CONDITIONS  │
                    └──────┬───────┘
                           ▼
┌──────────────┐    ┌──────────────┐   ?   ┌────────────┐
│   BELIEFS    │    │              │◄─────►│            │
│ EXPECTATIONS │───►│  HAPPINESS   │       │ MEDITATION │
│     AND      │    │              │       │            │
│    VALUES    │    └──────▲───────┘       └────────────┘
└──────────────┘           │
                    ┌──────┴───────┐
                    │              │
        ┌───────────┴──┐        ┌──┴─────────┐
        │  HYPOMANIA   │        │   DRUGS    │
        └──────────────┘        └────────────┘
```

The mood of happiness can be influenced by external conditions such as family, finance, work, friends, and personal freedom. Similarly, happiness can be altered directly by drugs or through natural swings in mood (e.g. hypomania). The exact effects of meditation, beliefs, expectations and values remain debatable.

drug-dependent contented majority and an embittered and occasionally depressed puritan minority.

So I suggest that happiness can be considered to be a mood, and a good mood tends to correlate with certain conditions in the brain, such as activation of the left frontal lobe and the easy supply of serotonin and dopamine. Can, then, markedly different causes (e.g. a steady friendship or a religious belief) cause the same sort of happiness that is caused by a drug or a natural state of hypomania? Yes, I think they can. In all cases we end up with the same or similar neuro-physiological condition.

Although there are many different external causes of happiness and unhappiness we can still compare them all for levels of *intensity*. Just like the music of Beethoven is different in quality from the sound of a road-drill we can nevertheless compare them for loudness. Just as we can physically measure decibels so we can, theoretically, measure the intensities of happiness and unhappiness, regardless of their different contents or origins. Furthermore, happiness and unhappiness really do seem to be on one dimension. Can we be both happy and unhappy, in a sustained manner, at the same time? Not really. Sometimes we can have ambivalent or mixed thoughts or feelings about somebody or something but these are *cognitive* or *emotional* states and are not quite the same as *mood*. The basic mood of happiness/unhappiness (or mania/depression) is unitary, although we can also be aroused and unaroused, and this dimension of arousal may alter the quality of our happiness. We might, for example, call unaroused happiness 'contentment' or 'serenity', and aroused happiness 'joy' or 'ecstasy'.

Is mania, then, supreme happiness? Not quite, because at such extremes of raised mood things begin to go wrong and the individual may have negative experiences including irritability, suspiciousness, delusions of persecution and even hallucinations. Even lower levels of mania, often called *hypomania*, although characteristically euphoric, are a form of happiness that is highly charged. Nothing is restful. The whole mind and body is in a highly aroused condition,

TABLE TWO

The two-way relationship between Mood and Experiences

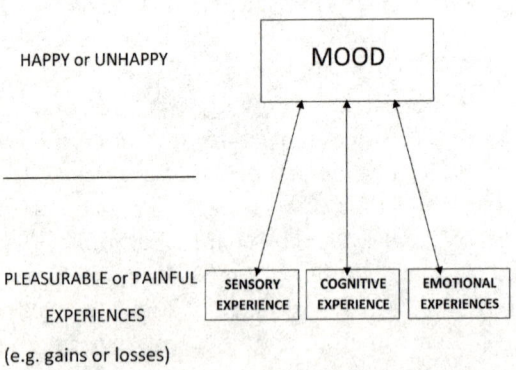

HAPPY or UNHAPPY → MOOD

PLEASURABLE or PAINFUL EXPERIENCES → SENSORY EXPERIENCE | COGNITIVE EXPERIENCE | EMOTIONAL EXPERIENCES
(e.g. gains or losses)

Sensory, cognitive and emotional experiences affect our mood. But mood, too, affects these experiences.

in association with raised nor-adrenaline. In both its forms, however, both as *ecstasy* and *serenity*, happiness can sometimes come and go unprompted by external events, just like a mood.

The current century has seen a sudden burgeoning of academic interest in the subject of happiness. Even the recession of 2008 seemingly intensified this interest. At this juncture a less materialistic attitude among the British was reported[12] as people spent less time on buying and more on volunteering, walking, bicycling and enjoying the environment. The old idea was revived that giving more back to the community promotes one's own happiness.

If the happiness of others is the aim of morality, then we now need to spend some time examining morality.

What Are the Foundations of Morality?

How does happiness fit in with morality? There is, of course, nothing that is 'self-evidently' right or wrong, as John Locke would have it. Without having to trust in the invention of a divine will, are there more down to earth reasons that justify morality? Are there moral foundations that are hard and unchallengeable? David Hume proposed that morality was founded not upon reason but upon passions or sentiments. One knows exactly what he was driving at. He was wanting to build upon the natural feelings of sympathy and compassion we have all felt when, for example, we have seen a starving child or a wounded animal. Such pain in others and our reactions to it are far more real foundations for ethics than are any allegations of divine will. Indeed, their reality is searing. Most humans do not have to be taught to want to help in such situations. We naturally want to reduce pain and restore happiness. Our compassion is instinctive. Perhaps, in order to create a satisfactory theory of ethics, the actions that flow naturally from such compassion just need to be universalised, made consistent and codified.

---

[12] Rachel Shields: *The Secret of* Happiness, *Independent on Sunday*, 15 August 2010

Doing Whatever We Want to Do

So why don't we just let go and act naturally? If our natural compassion drives us spontaneously into doing good then why not let it rip? Well, of course, not all of our passions are so morally positive. In fact most of our drives are selfish and some are actually harmful to others. We are a mixture of good and bad passions. So it does not follow that we ought always to do what our instincts tell us to do. All mammals, humans included, show a cocktail of drives ranging from nurturing and caring at one extreme to violent aggression and sadistic (in the human case) cruelty at the other. The sight of another's suffering can sometimes prompt feelings far more negative than compassion — even feelings of sadistic relish. The requirement is clearly to devise a moral system that encourages and cultivates the good impulses and holds the bad ones in check. How do we do it? Again, it is primarily a matter for the two powerful sources of approval — peer group approval and authority approval. We clearly need to construct a culture in which these two sources of approval are withheld from those who act violently or cruelly, and given to those who express compassion. In most Western societies, thankfully, we have this situation. There are, of course, gang cultures or hidden subcultures within most societies (e.g. in closed institutions such as some prisons, police stations, laboratories and slaughter houses) where subcultures exist which may tolerate or cultivate the opposite: where cruelty is approved or excused and compassion is ridiculed. We need to open up these secret enclaves, let in the light of publicity, install television cameras and subject them to wider cultural sanctions. Wherever there is secrecy within a society, watch out! These places can still become cancers of cruelty in the body of a civilised society.

Kantian Ethics

Immanuel Kant was so pessimistic about the cruel instincts of human beings that he insisted that morality had to be all about the imposition of strict rules. He was right that humankind's bullying, domineering, and teasing tendencies need to be suppressed and controlled not only by laws but by an internalised sense of duty. Kant was helpful in encouraging a respect for duty through his complex idea of the Categorical Imperative. But he went too far in his emphases. For Kant the core of ethics lies in our motives and not in what we actually do. He disliked the idea of the Golden Rule and the concept of benevolence. Even happiness left him cold. For Kant the only thing in itself that is good is 'good will'. Can a sadist then be left to torture people if he does it out of a peculiar sense of good will? In a sense, Hitler's policies were motivated by good will for the German nation, and by a sense of duty. So was Hitler morally alright? This cold lack of content in the Kantian system can make it appear quite ludicrous. Rather like Aristotle, Kant focused upon the *character and virtues of the moral agent* and not upon the consequences of the agent's actions upon others. One difference from Aristotle was that Kant wanted to see the *containment* of human drives whereas Aristotle believed that human drives should be *moderately satisfied*. Aristotle, of course, was focusing more upon what makes each of us feel contented (through our *telos* or the satisfaction of our natural drives such as hunger and so on) than promulgating a truly moral system indicating how we should behave towards *others*. The distinction between what makes *me* happy and what makes *others* happy is crucial. As I have already said, it is only when we are addressing the latter that we are truly talking about morality.

Kant's emphasis upon the importance of duty (regardless as to the actions this entailed) heralded much of the moral culture of nineteenth century Europe. Thousands, impelled by a highly developed sense of duty would build empires, work hard, eschew divorce, give money to the poor and fight bravely in bloody and often unjust wars. Kant subtly encouraged the idea that going against our own natures can be laudable. The good person has to act correctly according to 'reason' and 'good intention' and *not* impulse. So Kant helped perpetuate the puritanical and 'stiff upper lip' traditions in Europe that condemned the fleshly appetites and encouraged self-control. In psychological terms Sigmund Freud, without taking a strong moral position, would make a similar distinction between the *id* (our instincts) and the *super ego* (our conscience or sense of duty). Today this perennial tension between instincts and duties, between natural impulses and moral scruples, is sometimes described in terms of brain function: the struggle between 'emotional' hypothalamus and 'cognitive' frontal cortex. Scan research tends to support this. However it is described, this dichotomy is very much a part of human nature and Kant's contribution was to elevate the importance of our so-called rational or cognitive side and our sense of duty. His 'categorical imperative' urged that morality should be universal and that all human beings should be treated as ends in themselves, never merely as means. Sadly, Kant left out the other animals. It seems that he was so impressed by the power of cool reason that, on the assumption that other animals lacked such reason, he excluded them entirely. In the eyes of many Kant stood for the containment of selfish impulses.

Utilitarianism

The Utilitarians such as Jeremy Bentham and John Stuart Mill were far better psychologists than Kant and altogether more relaxed about human nature. Their whole emphasis was upon the *consequences* of actions. *Whatever increased the overall happiness of the greatest number was considered to be good.* By looking at the consequences of actions rather than concentrating upon the character of the moral agent the Utilitarians avoided all the confusions that the 'character' camp inevitably encounters. They tended to show their concern for the victims of actions rather than the perpetrators, and this was an important step away from the classical and Christian narrow obsession with the virtues of the agent. More specifically, their awareness of the fundamental importance of pain, pleasure and happiness gave secular morality a far firmer foundation. Furthermore, it allowed human instincts a proper status. The satisfaction of drives such as hunger, sex, envy and ambition were recognised as elemental sources of pleasures and happiness, just as their frustration was understood to be a potent source of pain. Whereas Kant's position was a strained and artificial one, that of the Utilitarians was far more relaxed and natural. They were prepared to 'go with the flow' of human nature.

Traditionally, most opposition to Utilitarianism has been based upon a misunderstanding — the idea that Utilitarians are seeking short term or 'scandalous' (sexual) pleasures. In fact Bentham and Mill were both clear that they were interested not in evanescent pleasures but in long-lasting happiness. Yet some critics, such as Matthieu Ricard, still persist in this rather puritanical misunderstanding.[13]

Utilitarianism versus Rights Theory

Two of the best known moral theories are concerned with happiness: one explicitly (Utilitarianism) and the other covertly (Rights Theory). Much fuss is made about the so-called clash between Utilitarian and Rights theories. Ethicists sometimes see the two schools of thought as being totally incompatible, the one claiming that the aim of morality is the 'greatest happiness of the greatest number', while the other seeing it all as a question of rights. In fact the two schools are far more compatible than some of their zealots seem to realise. Their differences are largely differences in language. My own theory of Painism actually builds a bridge between the two theories (see pp 62–89).

Utilitarianism made something of a comeback in the 1970s and 1980s under the influence of Peter Singer, and quite rightly. It was high time to revive Bentham's clear-sighted emphasis upon pains and pleasures, and of course, on happiness. Rights Theory today is also of great importance socially and politically in preserving and enhancing the status of the individual. Both theories, however, have their detractors. There are those who criticise Rights Theory because it provides no clear rules as to how

---

[13] Matthieu Ricard: *Happiness: A Guide to Developing Life's Most Important Skill*, Atlantic Books, p 247, 2003

conflicts between rights are to be resolved. There are also those, like myself, who criticise Utilitarianism because it does not take seriously 'the separateness of individuals'. My theory of Painism deals with both these problems. Rights to 'liberty, property, security and resistance to oppression' are all means to enhancing happiness, as are at least a hundred other rights. Some people attack Rights Theory as encouraging a selfish attitude towards society by demanding certain benefits for the individual without emphasising their duties or responsibilities. On the other side people promote the rights of the individual (or civil liberties) as a way to stand up against the encroachment of an over-powerful state. The individualism of Rights Theory seems to me to be correct although I dislike its potential selfishness. Painism blends the two into an altruistic form of individualism. (See Chapter 3.)

The Revival of Virtue Ethics

In view of the above it seems strange that there was a twentieth century revival of interest in Virtue Ethics — as shown by writers such as Elizabeth Anscombe, Alasdair MacIntyre and Philippa Foot. It is certainly true that virtues (as personality traits) predispose people to act in certain ways. Thus a just person is more likely than an unjust person to cause happiness to others. So it is a good idea to encourage people to become just and indeed to train them in justice as Aristotle suggested. But this is surely only because such conduct causes happiness for others. In other words, *virtues are merely means to good ends*. When the Virtue Ethicists suggest that *who* you are matters more than what you *do*, they go too far. They have got their priorities wrong. Of course we are concerned about the wellbeing of moral agents as well as that of their victims — but that should be a concern with their happiness and not with their virtue.

When faced with a particular action — for example helping an old lady to cross the road — why should the motives or character of the helper be of moral importance? What really matters morally is the *wellbeing of the old lady*. A psychologist might want to understand the helper's motives but such motives are of no account *morally* speaking.

There are two big issues here. The first is about *who is the focus of attention* in moral questions. Should it be the moral agent or should it be his victims? The second is about *the ultimate nature of goodness*. Does it consist in virtue or in happiness? In each case the former answer appears nebulous whereas the latter seems real. For this reason I focus upon the *happiness of victims* rather than upon the *virtue of moral agents*. Aristotle actually complicated the picture by saying that there are two types of virtue: *moral virtues* (such as temperance, modesty, righteous indignation, courage, liberality, magnificence, magnanimity, proper ambition, patience, truthfulness, wittiness and friendliness) and *intellectual virtues* (such as skill, intelligence, wisdom, understanding, judgement and prudence). Cicero simplified these into the four 'cardinal virtues' of courage, temperance, wisdom and justice. One of the problems with Virtue Ethics is that virtues, like rights, can more or less be snatched out of the air. Anyone can invent virtues. They are rarely justified in terms of any more fundamental quality such as happiness. Hitler, for example, thought that anti-semitism was a virtue. Some have favoured chastity, extravagance or even cruelty as virtues. Virtues have an arbitrary quality. Christianity opted for faith, hope and charity. I do not wish to disparage such virtues. But if they are recognised as being only a means to an end, the end being the happiness of others, then we can see that any such personality traits can indeed be useful. The greatest of them, however, would surely be a feeling for the wellbeing of others; in other words love or charity or, as we might call it today, empathy or compassion, some of which is learned but much of which is innate. (Just a word here about the terms 'sympathy' and 'empathy' which tend to be used interchangeably. Strictly speaking empathy is more general than is sympathy, denoting 'the ability to share and understand another person's feelings' of any sort (*Chambers Dictionary*). Sympathy on the other hand focuses upon the 'sadness or suffering of others' (*Chambers Dictionary*) and sometimes implies affection or support for them.

Sympathy derives from the Greek *syn* meaning 'with' and *pathos* meaning 'suffering'.)

As I have suggested, much of the confusion in the subject of ethics generally has been due to an uncertainty about whether we are talking about the right way to behave towards others, or about the right way to live in order to find *our own* happiness. These are two entirely separate issues. Aristotle muddled them up completely causing centuries of chaos. Surely, the question of how I have to behave in order to have an enjoyable or pleasant life is simply a matter of economics and psychology. I need sufficient funds in order to be able to eat, sleep and keep warm, and I need to act so that I feel fulfilled, have friends and avoid all other sources of unhappiness as much as possible. (See pp ... and Chapter 4) As I have argued, morality is quite different — and often at odds with the above. *It is about how I should treat others*. This is one reason why the modern escape from Virtue Ethics is so salutary. At last we can see clearly what our moral objectives are: they are all about improving the lives of *others*, not of ourselves. This raises the question of who do we mean by 'others'? Are foreigners, women and animals to be excluded, as Aristotle would have it? Of course not. If happiness is the ultimate objective then we should include all those who are capable of experiencing happiness. Speciesism, like racism, ageism, sexism and classism has no place in a modern morality.

Bringing It All Together

From this short introduction it can be seen that Western society in the last five hundred years has been influenced strongly by Christian ethics and by at least four secular ways of thinking about morality — Virtue Ethics, Kantian Theory, Utilitarianism and Rights Theory. Despite the faltering revival of interest in Virtue Ethics and the lingering influence of the Kantian concept of duty, the two principal ethical theories governing the whole of secular Western thinking and policy over many decades have been Utilitarianism and Rights Theory. These two theories, although rarely articulated with clarity, now underlie most of Western governance and of democracy itself. Yet often they are claimed to be in irreconcilable conflict. Reconciling these two theories, and discounting the other secular theories, is what this book is about.

In this first chapter I have raised questions about morality and happiness and have suggested some of the problems that exist in current thinking. The next two chapters on speciesism and painism are intended to begin to provide answers to these problems.

I confess to being the creator of these two neologisms — *speciesism*, which is a prejudice like sexism or racism and *painism* which is my moral theory. I apologise that these 'isms' are so different in meaning - the first denoting a prejudice and the latter a theory. I am against speciesism but all in favour of painism! This is not a science book, but it *is* informed by science; it reflects my belief in science and that there is such a thing as truth. It deals with the interface between science and ethics. The book is also speculative because I believe in informed speculation as an essential part of the creative and scientific processes.

CHAPTER 2

Speciesism

Introduction

As a child some of my best friends were animals. Dogs, cats and birds. I even had a monkey living in my bedroom. It never crossed my mind that these individuals, although obviously different in appearance from me, were unfeeling machines. Of course not. I knew they felt anger, joy and fear much as I did. Above all, I realised that they could suffer too. We understood each other perfectly well. Later, I was brought up to shoot at birds and rabbits for sport but always felt a horror at what I was doing. I enjoyed the excitement of the chase but at the same time hated the pain and death that I was causing. When I was twenty-one I gave up such cruelties. Then, as a young psychologist at Cambridge I was shocked to see rats and monkeys with holes in their heads where their brains had been experimentally damaged. When I questioned whether this was morally right, people looked at me strangely as if I was mad. What was the justification for putting our own species into an entirely separate moral category I asked them? I could not see the logic in it. One day in 1969 I indignantly protested against an otter hunt in Dorset and then, from the hospital where I worked in Oxford, I wrote angry letters to a national newspaper attacking vivisection. The reactions to both these actions were explosive. I found myself organising numerous protest events against otter hunts as well as street demonstrations against animal experimentation, and appearing frequently on radio and television, once with the novelist Brigid Brophy on the first-ever televised debate about the then almost forgotten subject of animal rights, at the end of 1970.

That same year I coined the term *speciesism* when in my bath one day, and used it as the title for two editions of a leaflet that were circulated around Oxford in which I urged people to 'extend our concern about elementary rights to the nonhumans' and, in the following year, I referred to speciesism in my chapter on animal experimentation in the ground-breaking *Animals, Men and Morals* that was edited and published by Stanley and Roslind Godlovitch and John Harris in 1971. Since that time, speciesism has become part of the philosophical vernacular, gaining a life of its own and several new meanings. My initial intention was to use the term as a psychological tool with which to prize open established habits of thought and to fully extend the scope of ethics to cover the treatment of nonhuman animals. The analogy with racism and sexism I hoped would force many who had not deeply considered the condition of nonhumans to pause and realise that it should be a serious political and ethical issue in our anthropocentric society. In 1970 the words racism and sexism themselves had only recently gained widespread currency.

Consciousness

There are still a few writers who assert that the human is the only species which is conscious. Well, all I can say is, good luck to them. I know no serious cognitive scientist under the age of sixty who believes this. It is certainly impossible to prove. (I can't *prove* that anyone other than myself is conscious — you could all be lying robots!) What causes consciousness is, of course, a mystery. But few scientists today would deny that it is a function of the awake brain. Consciousness emerges from the pulsating brain as mysteriously as electricity emerges from the copper wires of a spinning dynamo. There is no 'centre' for consciousness within the brain but it is certainly correlated with activity in the brain's cortex. As all mammals, and many other animals, have brains that have similar cortices, containing similar chemical neurotransmitters, it is reasonable to assume that these species are also conscious. Of course, what really matters in morality is not consciousness generally but the consciousness of *pain*; and such painience, being of special evolutionary value, is highly likely to be widespread in nature. Painience is no respecter of species.

Definitions of Speciesism

In 1972 I had called speciesism 'illogical and totally selfish' and in 1974 argued that:

> to say one species has a right to exploit the others is to be guilty of the prejudice of speciesism, just as to argue that one race has a right to subordinate another race is racism.

I went on in 1975, in my book *Victims of Science*, to use the term speciesism to describe:

> The widespread discrimination that is practised by man against the other species ... speciesism and racism are both forms of prejudice that are based upon appearances ...

Peter Singer subtly altered this in his *Animal Liberation* of 1975, defining speciesism as:

> A prejudice or attitude of bias in favour of the interests of members of one's own species against those of members of other species.

This definition stipulates that the bias in speciesism is only for one's own species, so, if I favour the interests of dogs over cats, I appear not to be a speciesist in Singer's reckoning, nor if I favour the interests of, say, horses against human interests. But if a chimpanzee puts the interests of his troop before that of a troop of baboons then that could be speciesism.

These seem to be differences of minor importance yet they have provoked debate and heralded a host of new definitions. In 1985 the *Oxford English Dictionary* stated that speciesism is:

discrimination against or exploitation of certain animal species by human beings, based on an assumption of mankind's superiority.

This formulation adds exploitation to the description. (Racism had already acquired the double meaning of denoting actual physical exploitation (e.g. black slavery) as well as a belief or attitude.) This definition of speciesism also spells out the rationale for such behaviour as being a belief in human superiority. What form this superiority takes or how it justifies speciesism is not explained.

This emphasis on the assumption of human superiority is also picked up by the *Chambers Concise Dictionary* definition of speciesism in 2001:

> the assumption that humans are superior to all other species of animals and are, therefore, justified in exploiting them for their own use.

Collins English Dictionary puts it the other way around, emphasising animal inferiority, thus defining speciesism in 2007 as:

> a belief of humans that all other species of animals are inferior and may, therefore, be used for human benefit without regard to the suffering inflicted.

This mentions suffering explicitly and is thus in line with my own philosophical emphasis and that of Singer.

American definitions include *Webster's World Dictionary* of 2005:

> discrimination against or exploitation of animals based on the assumption that humans are superior to and more important than all other species.

This is very similar to those of the *Oxford* and *Chambers* dictionaries (above), whereas that of the *American Heritage Dictionary* varies by mentioning cruelty, defining speciesism in 2009 as:

> human intolerance or discrimination on the basis of species, especially as manifested by cruelty to or exploitation of animals.

Philosophers' definitions of speciesism have introduced new features. In 1994 Simon Blackburn in the *Oxford Dictionary of Philosophy* describes speciesism as:

> by analogy with racism or sexism, the improper stance of refusing respect to the lives, dignity, rights or needs of animals of other than the human species.

Thomas Mautner in the 1996 edition of the *Penguin Dictionary of Philosophy* prefers:

> the theory and practice that assigns a privileged position to mankind, such that we are entitled to treat members of other species in a way in which it would be wrong to treat members of our own ...

whereas Jennifer Bothamley in the 1993 *Dictionary of Theories* suggests that speciesism is:

> the doctrine that certain species are innately superior to others; and is used especially to describe the exploitation of lower species by humans.

In the *Encyclopedia of Animal Rights and Animal Welfare* edited by Marc Bekoff in 1998 I pointed out that there are at least two separate meanings of speciesism. The first describes the exploitation of nonhumans justified on the grounds that they supposedly lack certain qualities alleged to have moral importance (such as high intelligence, reason, autonomy, a moral sense or a soul), whereas the second describes the exploitation of nonhumans as being justified purely on the grounds that they are of a nonhuman species. An illustration of the latter would be to approve severe experiments on an intelligent chimpanzee but not upon an irreversibly brain-dead human. In the latter case it is principally the *species-difference itself* that is taken as justification. I called the latter usage strong speciesism and the former weak speciesism.

Many other uses are now found conversationally. Sometimes speciesism is attributed to nonhuman agents as when, for example, dogs are said to be especially hostile to cats. The term has also been used to describe attitudes towards humans, as when a human loner is alleged to dislike his fellows and prefer the company of nonhumans.

Sometimes speciesism is also used to describe a positive rather than a negative attitude as when dolphins are alleged to have rescued humans from danger while ignoring other species in peril. So we can see that in addition to the weak and strong versions, there are four other dimensions along which the use of the term speciesism can vary:

- whether it is used to describe a belief or a practice
- whether the agent is said to be human or nonhuman
- whether it is used to describe discrimination against nonhumans or against humans
- whether it is used to describe positive or negative discrimination

Arguably, whenever a nonhuman shows a preference for her own species this could be called speciesism. Carnivores, for example, often refrain from eating members of their own species. Such discrimination presumably is based upon instinct rather than culture or a consciously held belief. Does this prevent such behaviour being described as speciesist? If the sustained conscious belief in one's own species' superiority is regarded as an essential component in the definition of speciesism, then it is doubtful that speciesism can be said to exist in other species at all. So it may be inappropriate to talk of speciesism in that sense as manifesting in any species other than humankind. For most purposes it is probably expedient to use the term speciesism as a description of negative human discrimination or exploitation against members of other species. The analogy with racism and sexism remains psychologically important whether it is explicit or implied. Speciesism is sometimes based upon no particular philosophy or upon the unthinking assumption that the species-difference is sufficient grounds, or upon a claim that some form of alleged human superiority justifies such prejudice.

Manifestations of Speciesism

The origins of speciesism are lost in the mists of time. Humankind has clearly eaten and exploited other animals ever since our species evolved. Some other primate species today are predominantly vegetarian but all tend behaviourally to distinguish between their own species and others. Nevertheless before we assume that in some sense all species are naturally speciesist we should note (a) that violence often occurs between members of the same species, and (b) that species sometimes show a considerable positive interest in members of other species as, for example, in the play and friendship that occurs in the wild between young chimpanzees and baboons. No scientist has yet been able to test other species for the presence or otherwise of speciesist beliefs. Yet the common experience of close relationships between members of different domesticated species, and between humans and their pets, suggests that strong bonds of affection frequently occur across the species boundary. Even in the wild, dolphins have been recorded as protecting humans from shark attacks and sometimes adults of one species may foster the young of another species, and such adoptees sometimes grow up to behave as if they considered themselves members of their adoptive species.

Archaeological evidence suggests that our human ancestors may have perceived themselves to be closer to the other animals than we do in modern times. Cave paintings from some 20,000 years ago indicate how our ancestors chose nonhuman animals to be their principal subjects, apparently expressing a religious admiration for these animals' strength and beauty. The depiction of other humans in such paintings is secondary and hunting scenes are relatively rare.

Animals certainly feature widely in early religions such as the Egyptian where the gods were represented as having human bodies and animal heads. In mythology, too, the species boundary is crossed to produce hybrid monsters, and in some tribal belief systems, even today, the spirits of animals are considered to be powerful influences or to have important totemic significance. Nearly all the great religions at some stage in their development included animal sacrifice, indicating that animals were seen as of great intrinsic value, approaching that of humans. In antiquity the continuum between life forms was accepted and, in Buddhism and Jainism, overtly respected. In many cultures the human species was not regarded as being entirely different in kind from the other animals. Indeed, human-animal hybrids were frequently depicted in legend, and human and animal souls were believed to move across the divide after death, individual animals being reborn as humans, and humans as animals. In Judaeo-Christian cultures, however, a distinction between humankind and the animals was emphasised based upon the notion that only humankind was, allegedly, made in the image of God. After the fourteenth century AD the perceived elevation of the human species again increased in Europe, reaching a speciesist nadir around 1600 AD at a time when animals were mercilessly hunted and baited for sport, tormented in the preparation of food and nailed to boards to be vivisected.[1]

Manifestations of speciesism in action have varied over the years, following both fashion and changes in technology. Animal protection organisations customarily divide their concerns into four major welfare categories — that of wild, farm, laboratory and companion animals. (Animals used in entertainment is an optional fifth category.) For example, in 2009 the animal welfare policies of the Royal Society for the Prevention of Cruelty to Animals (RSPCA) (the world's oldest and largest animal protection organisation) were thus divided. These headings covered some forty areas of suffering caused by human agency. Such manifestations of speciesism include genetic engineering, the patenting of animals, the breeding of abnormalities into animals, animals in zoos, surgical mutilations, the use of animal organs for transplantation, the use of animals in education, behavioural experiments, animals in captivity,

---

[1] Richard D Ryder: *Animal Revolution: Changing Attitudes Towards Speciesism*, Basil Blackwell, Oxford, 1989; 2nd Edition, Berg, Oxford, 2000.

performing animals, rodeos, dog racing, falconry, bullfighting, animals in fiestas, animals as prizes, fur production, hunting with hounds, shooting for sport and other purposes, angling and other forms of fishing, horse racing, show jumping, equine riding, all forms of slaughter, the rearing of poultry, calves, pigs and other food animals, egg production, livestock markets, transportation, the treatment of casualty farm animals, painful and often unnecessary experiments on animals, the supply and care of laboratory animals, the use of snares and traps, poisons, trade in wildlife and the killing of whales and seals. Nowhere would such exploitative treatment of human animals pass without censure in the world today. The fact that such practices continue to be tolerated is therefore evidence of widespread institutionalised speciesism.

Religious Views

Ethical opposition to the killing of animals goes back many centuries and at least to the time of Gotama Buddha in the sixth century BC. Buddha, deeply concerned about suffering, turned against the contemporary practice of animal sacrifice and three centuries later his follower, the Emperor Asoka in India, issued decrees protective of animals. Although Buddhism sees animals as being below humans in the hierarchy of the chain of being, it asserts that the killing of living creatures is a violation of basic moral law. It is wrong because it is associated with greed and hatred and because it has harmful consequences for the doer. Although the perceived continuum between human and animal is reinforced by the belief that one form can be reincarnated into the other in future lives, Buddhism still views all animals as being inferior to humans and so, in this limited sense, remains speciesist.

Jainism was developed in India by Mahavira, probably a contemporary of Buddha around 500 BC, and focuses much more precisely upon the principle of consciousness. Nothing in the Universe is deemed to be without some degree of sentience. The most fundamental moral principle of Jainism is *Ahimsa* or the non-harming of highly sentient beings. Meat-eating is therefore strictly prohibited and great care is taken to avoid the harming or killing of even primitive creatures such as insects. Yet although some modern writers have asserted that *Ahimsa* is related to the occurrence of suffering among living things, its ultimate justification is not that it respects the animals but that it raises the moral stature of the human practitioner. So even here, in Jainism, there is a speciesist element.

In Islam it is believed that God created both human and nonhuman and gave people power over the animals. Yet to treat animals badly is to disobey God's will. It is wrong to hunt merely for pleasure, to cause animals to fight each other or to molest them unnecessarily. There are many reports of the Prophet's concern not only over the killing of animals but about the causing of unnecessary suffering.

Judaism recognises that animals are part of God's creation, but gives dominion or at least stewardship to humans. Many rules appear in the Old Testament that are protective of animals although animal sacrifice — ironically believed to be a means of expunging the stain of human sin — was practised almost obsessively until less than two thousand years ago, and the temple in Jerusalem was said to run with blood. Yet Hillel and other great teachers emphasised the Golden Rule — 'What you dislike don't do to others; that is the whole Torah', and Maimonides in the twelfth century asserted that it is wrong to cause animals pain in slaughter. The very foundations of Judaism (and Christianity), however, remain speciesist in that animals are said to be put upon Earth for human use, and a central teaching of the Torah is that only humankind is created in the image of God.

Little in the New Testament suggests that Christianity sees matters differently. Other than remarking that even sparrows are of importance to God, Jesus is not recorded as having mentioned animals in a moral context. He allegedly sent demons into a herd of swine and seemed unconcerned when the pigs threw themselves over a cliff. Maybe this impression of callousness is because the gospel writers did not believe the subject was important or because they felt they had to distinguish the new religion from cults which had worshipped animals or animal-shaped idols (e.g. the golden calf) or because they sought to defend it against actual contemporary accusations that Christianity was associated with donkey worship. Recently scholars have suggested that the buying and selling of animals in the temple for the purpose of sacrifice was the chief commercial operation conducted there. Indeed, I have proposed that his disgust with this bloody exploitation of animals was the real reason for Jesus' strangely violent outburst in the temple and the arrest that led to his execution. By preaching the gospel of loving one's neighbour and even one's enemy, Christianity certainly eroded some of the basic cruelties of Roman culture, among them the colossal exploitation of animals in the arenas of the Roman Empire. Although there is little else recorded in writing on the treatment of animals in the early Christian era, the lives of the early saints are revealing. These celebrities and role models of the period are frequently depicted as showing mercy to animals, sharing their lives with them and even rescuing them from cruel exploitation at the hands of hunters. Indeed, until the death of St Francis of Assisi in 1226 a concern for the animals was almost a hallmark of saintliness all over Europe, and especially in the Eastern church. Yet other great teachers of the church were having none of this. St Paul had argued that Deuteronomy's injunction about not muzzling oxen was not for the benefit of the oxen but for human benefit. St Thomas Aquinas (born 1225) agreed:

> God's purpose in recommending kind treatment of the brute Creation is to dispose men to pity and tenderness towards one another.

Aquinas followed the newly available pagan teachings of Aristotle (384–322 BC) who had taught the inferior moral status of women, slaves and animals. Together Aristotle and Aquinas, both of whom hugely influenced the moral development of Europe from the early Renaissance onwards, can now be recognised as leaders of the cult of speciesism as, later, was René Descartes (1596–1650) who viewed animals as unfeeling machines. And speciesism became a cult to the extent that some highminded puritans seemed to equate civilisation itself as a process of moving away from the 'animal' parts of our human nature; a fear of sexuality probably forming the main component of this.

Attacks on Speciesism

The eighteenth century, however, saw a widespread turning against speciesism expressed by writers and intellectuals, especially in the northern Protestant countries of Europe. In the following century such sentiments were converted into legislation and the establishment of animal protection organisations all over Europe, North America and in some parts of the British Empire. Those fighting speciesism were often the same individuals who fought against slavery and campaigned for humanitarian, child-protection, feminist and political reforms generally. Examples are William Wilberforce, Fowell Buxton, Richard Martin, Lord Shaftesbury and John Stuart Mill. The abhorrence of pain was their common feature.

Many Victorians still feared their own animal natures and so found Darwinism particularly upsetting. Yet Queen Victoria herself and many social reformers of the period promoted the new animal welfare sympathies until the two World Wars temporarily stopped the progress of the movement in the first part of the following century.[2] Nowhere is this more clearly seen than in the attitudes of leading lawyers. In a pivotal case between the National Anti Vivisection Society of London and the Inland Revenue Commissioners, speciesism was reinforced. In an influential judgement that affected the status of animal charities for many decades and was reported in the *All England Law Reports* for 19 July 1947, Lord Wright concluded:

---

[2] Richard D Ryder: *Animal Revolution: Changing Attitudes Towards Speciesism* Basil Blackwell, Oxford, 1989; 2nd Edition, Berg, Oxford, 2000.

The life and happiness of human beings must be preferred to that of animals. Mankind, of whatever race or breed, is on a higher plane and a different level from even the highest of the animals who are our friends, helpers and companions. No-one faced with the decision to choose between saving a man or an animal could hesitate to save the man.

It can be seen that this classic speciesist statement is unsupported by proper argument. The morally superior status of the human species that allegedly justifies putting human interests before all others, is not rationally argued but merely *asserted* on the claim that human beings are 'on a higher plane and a different level' from other animals.

The revolutionary decade of the 1960s, that spotlighted and attacked both racism and sexism, also introduced a new concern for the protection of animals. In 1969 I began to write letters in the press attacking both hunting and vivisection and in the following year published two editions of a leaflet entitled *Speciesism* which went as follows:

Speciesism

Since Darwin, scientists have agreed that there is no 'magical' essential difference between human and other animals, biologically-speaking. Why then do we make an almost total distinction morally? If all organisms are on one physical continuum, then we should also be on the same moral continuum.

The word 'species', like the word 'race', is not precisely definable. Lions and tigers can interbreed. Under special laboratory conditions it may soon prove possible to mate a gorilla with a professor of biology — will the hairy offspring be kept in a cage or a cradle?

It is customary to describe Neanderthal Man as a separate species from ourselves, one especially equipped for Ice-Age survival. Yet most archæologists now believe that this nonhuman creature practised ritual burial and possessed a larger brain than we do. Suppose that the elusive Abominable Snowman, when caught, turns out to be the last survivor of this

Neanderthal species, would we give him a seat at the UN or would we implant electrodes in his super-human brain?

I use these hypothetical, but possible examples, to draw attention to the illogicality of our present moral position as regards experiments with animals.

About 5,000,000 laboratory animals, more and more of them Primates like ourselves, are killed every year in the UK alone, and numbers are now escalating out of control. There are only 12 Home Office Inspectors.

Quite apart from the right to live, one clear moral criterion is suffering, the suffering of imprisonment, fear and boredom as well as physical pain.

If we assume that suffering is a function of the nervous system then it is illogical to argue that other animals do not suffer in a similar way to ourselves – it is precisely because some other animals have nervous systems so like our own that they are so extensively studied.

The only arguments in favour of painful experiments on animals are: 1) that the advancement of knowledge justifies all evils – well does it? 2) that possible benefits for our own species justify mistreatment of other species – this may be a fairly strong argument when it applies to experiments where the chances of suffering are minimal and the probability of aiding applied medicine is great, but even so it is still just 'speciesism', and as such it is a selfish emotional argument rather than a reasoned one.

If we believe it is wrong to inflict suffering upon innocent human animals then it is only logical, phylogenetically-speaking, to extend our concern about elementary rights to the non-human animals as well. **Do not be afraid to express your views**. *Contact MPs, professors, editors about this increasingly important moral issue.*

Later, I elaborated on my concept of speciesism in a series of pamphlets published in Edinburgh. In the first, *A Scientist Speaks on the Extensive Use of Animals in Non-Medical Research* (1972), I wrote:

Since Darwin we have, most of us, acknowledged our kinship with the other animals. We see ourselves as the Naked Ape—a member of the Primate Order, an animal among other animals. Why then do we put ourselves into an entirely privileged moral position? Where is the logic to this? Is there any? I don't think there is. If, as all scientists believe, we are all, animals and men, on the same continuum biologically, then surely we should be on the same continuum morally. Admittedly, we are on average the most intelligent species, but does that give us the right to exploit and torture the other species? If so, how about other less-intelligent individuals of our own species—do we have the right to experiment on children, subnormals or the old and senile? I have seen some human individuals in many respects less intelligent than a clever chimpanzee—and I say this as a psychologist—but should we feel we have a right to test weed-killers upon them?

We have no good scientific reason to believe that other animals do not suffer and die like ourselves. So if we believe that it is wrong to inflict pain on an innocent human creature, it should logically follow that it is wrong to do the same to any other species. What is the difference between species anyway? It may surprise the non-scientists to learn that the dividing line between species is *not* clearly drawn at all—lions and tigers can interbreed and so can their hybrids. And many interbreedings between monkey species have been recorded. There is no hard and fast line between us and the rest of the animal kingdom. Why then should we give ourselves rights under the law which we totally fail to accord to the other species? I regard such speciesism as being a very similar form of prejudice to racism—it is illogical and totally selfish.

In a later pamphlet entitled *Speciesism: The Ethics of Vivisection*, based upon a paper given to the London Medical Group in 1974, I referred to Jeremy Bentham and founded my remarks upon the findings of Charles Darwin and a need for the evolution of ethics itself. I argued that because there is good evidence that members of other species can suffer pain they should be included within all moral calculations. Simple arithmetic sums of pains and pleasures across individuals are not, however, acceptable in such calculations. The experience of each individual is of paramount importance. (See Chapter 3 *Painism*) When did physical differences (as between species) justify a moral prejudice? I cited Hitler and his prejudice against certain racial features and the defence used by Nazi doctors who had experimented upon Jewish prisoners:

> Is the species gap different in quality than the race gap? There are marked physical differences between the races. Does that justify a Hottentot surgeon experimenting on an unwilling Englishman? Did that justify slavery? To say one species has a right to exploit the others is to be guilty of the prejudice of speciesism, just as to argue that one race has a right to subordinate another race is racism. Racism and speciesism stand together as two similar forms of selfishness and discrimination—and together, in my opinion, they stand condemned. The words 'race' and 'species' have, after all, been used interchangeably and some geneticists have questioned whether the races of mankind could not better be called species or sub-species.

I went on to question the definitions and moral significance of race and species. Other Primates species could interbreed so what would happen if humans interbred with another primate? Would such a hybrid be sent to school or would it be vivisected? What would happen if super-powerful aliens from outer space landed on Earth and ordered all students to report for painful vivisection? How would we argue against their speciesist justifications? The arguments against the use of sentient animals in research were as valid as those against using children or members of other races. Vivisectors were in the same moral position as slavers who had justified black slavery on the grounds that white people's interests were paramount. Saying that differences in intelligence justify such exploitation is no better. There may be many such differences between species but none are morally relevant. The only commonality that matters is the capacity for suffering:

> Surely if we are all God's creatures, if all animal species are capable of feeling, if we are all evolutionary relatives, if all animals are on the same biological continuum, then also we should all be on the same *moral* continuum — and if it is wrong to inflict suffering upon an innocent and unwilling human, then it is wrong to do it to another species. To ignore this logic is to risk being guilty of the prejudice of Speciesism.

At the time these opinions received support from several Oxford luminaries including Iris Murdoch, Desmond Morris and Richard Dawkins, the latter emphasising that speciesism 'has no proper basis in evolutionary biology'.[3]

Why, then, have nonhuman animals so far failed to attain the same sort of legal standing as members of our own species? Why is it that, after centuries of rational argument in support of animal liberation, often by outstanding philosophers, have nonhumans continued to be almost universally tyrannized by humans? Is it just that they cannot campaign for their own rights? No, I think it is more than this. Humans are fairly omnivorous and some humans crave meat as fiercely as they crave sex.

Whether this is an acquired addiction or, for some at least, an innate need, is unknown. For some people vegetarianism for long periods is an easy choice, whereas for others abstention from meat is as hard as giving up cocaine. *Some of these people vigorously oppose raising the legal status of animals precisely because they fear enforced vegetarianism.* Is the continued humane rearing and slaughter of nonhumans for food to be allowed to sabotage the greater and wider admission of animals into the moral and legal in-group? I do not feel it should. Whereas killing humans for food will always be wrong because it creates fear and grief among other humans, I do not believe these problems generally apply in the case of nonhumans. In other words, I believe it *is* possi-

---

[3] Dawkins, Richard: *The Selfish Gene*, Open University Press, 1976; see also *The Blind Watchmaker*, Longman, 1986

ble to continue to raise the legal and moral status of nonhumans while still allowing some animals to be eaten. Natural deaths can, after all, be painful whereas, with proper care, rearing and slaughter can be without fear or distress of any sort. Sooner or later death is inevitable. It is pain, not death, that we should be strenuously opposing.

Philosophical Opposition to Speciesism

Early attacks on animal exploitation used terms such as animal rights (from circa 1683), liberties (1641), animal welfare, animal protection and animal liberation. In the nineteenth century the term zoophilism was introduced to describe a positive attitude towards the moral position of animals. From 1970 the word speciesism made the contemporary comparison with racism and sexism and turned the focus of attention onto the prejudice of the exploiter. Whereas speciesism does not in itself usually denote a philosophical position, unless expressed through anthropocentrism, the opposition to speciesism often does so. Nevertheless, a few philosophers have tried to defend speciesism. Peter Carruthers, for example, has argued from a contract theory position claiming that animals lack moral status because they cannot make a contract with us. He admits that neither can retarded nor very young humans make contracts but argues that we must still give these humans moral status or we would be on a slippery slope to abusing humans generally. R.G. Frey has denied that animals have rights on the standard Utilitarian grounds that the greater good (i.e. the total of all benefits to all those affected by an action) must be allowed to overrule the rights of the individual. If this is the case then presumably he must apply this rule to human individuals also.

In general the arguments in support of the prejudice of speciesism are unconvincing. They usually take the form of claims that humans (even neonatal and irreversibly brain-dead humans) have certain actual or potential qualities (such as rationality, a soul, autonomy, intelligence or a moral sense) that put all humans into a superior moral category, separate from all other animals, who are claimed (without much evidence) not to have many of these qualities. The argument then jumps to the assumption that because humans allegedly are in this special category it follows that we have certain privileges, interests or rights above those of all other species. No good reasons are given for this assumption. Speciesists fail to demonstrate why these qualities (such as rationality, a soul, autonomy, intelligence or a moral sense) are themselves morally relevant. Most modern philosophers since Bentham have doubted it. If true, would it follow that greater rights should therefore be given to humans who are especially rational, soulful, autonomous, intelligent or morally sensible? Should we, for example, put priests and academics on a pedestal and accord them a higher moral status than ordinary human beings? No, I believe the only morally relevant quality is the capacity to feel pain — that is the capacity to feel any sort of suffering whether it is cognitive, affective or sensory. Some have argued that only human animals are 'persons' and that it is this personhood that bestows moral standing Well, what is it other than painience that qualifies an individual for personhood? The central issue is pain itself rather than the differing vehicles of pain. Thus any painient individual has moral standing and their pains deserve equal consideration with the pains of every other painient individual, regardless of species. So X amount of pain in an elephant or a porpoise matters equally with X amount of pain in a university professor. There is no requirement to treat the elephant, the porpoise and the professor exactly the same because their needs are different. So feeding the same edible leaves to a porpoise or a professor as we give to an elephant would be as pointless as offering the elephant and porpoise dining rights in college. But painism does require us to treat equal quantities of pain equally.

After the revival of intellectual interest in the treatment of nonhuman animals in the 1960s three ethical positions were eventually developed in opposition to the prejudice of speciesism. They were based upon Utilitarian, Rights Theory and Painist principles respectively:

Utilitarian Comment

The Utilitarian opposition to speciesism has been eloquently led by Peter Singer who was a graduate student in Oxford at the time when the pioneering Oxford group were circulating leaflets, organising demonstrations against otter hunting, protesting against animal experimentation, and when the Oxford philosophers John Harris and Stanley and Roslind Godlovitch were editing and publishing *Animals, Men and Morals* in 1971. I had coined and published the term *speciesism* in early 1970 and I mentioned it in my contribution to their book as I did on television and in several leaflets in the early 1970s, while Singer employed the term throughout his *Animal Liberation* of 1975, with some twenty references in the index and incorporating it into the title or subtitle of two of its six chapters. Singer must, therefore, take much credit for helping to popularise the term I had invented, especially in America. In Europe, Canada and Australia I discussed speciesism in over fifty radio and television interviews and in written pieces and lectures, also attacking the prejudice from a broadly Utilitarian angle.

Singer's basic proposal is to include all sentient animals within the Utilitarian canon. This had already been proposed by Jeremy Bentham and John Stuart Mill — but it was a proposal that was constantly overlooked by their followers, whether political or academic. Utilitarianism proposes, according to Mill, that 'actions are right in proportion as they tend to promote happiness, wrong as they tend to produce the reverse of happiness'[4] and according to Bentham 'the proper end of action is to achieve the greatest happiness of the greatest number'. Singer's version is a form of Utilitarianism where happiness is measured by preferences. As it turns out these can often be measured experimentally in animals by, for example, offering hens various forms of accommodation and observing which they prefer, as was done by Marion Dawkins in Oxford in the 1970s. Jeremy Bentham in 1789 had compared the position of animals to

---

[4] John Stuart Mill, *Essay on Liberty*, J. Gray (Ed), Open University Press, 1991

that of black slaves and children concluding that in the case of animals:

> the question is not, Can they *reason*? Nor can they *talk*? But *can they suffer*?[5]

The underlying analogy between speciesism, racism and ageism is, therefore, long established.

Comment from Rights Theory

The second great ethical system that embraces the animals is Rights Theory and here the modern leader has been Tom Regan. Regan, too, passed through Oxford at the time when animal activists were drawing attention to the cause and, on his return to America, he began to extend Rights Theory to include the nonhuman animals.

Rights Theory has developed over many years and has provided driving ethics for political and social revolution and reform, Thomas Paine himself expressing a concern for animals. Acceptable in America, where rights formed a basis for the United States Bill of Rights, the term rights has had suspect connotations in Europe, associated as it was with the bloodshed and extremism of the French Revolution and its Declaration of the Rights of Man and the Citizen in 1789. In Britain neither revolution was welcomed politically and for this reason the use of the word rights never gained general acceptance until the end of the twentieth century. Even Bentham rejected the tendency to describe rights as if they are natural phenomena that have an objective existence like rocks or trees, describing natural rights as 'nonsense upon stilts'. Rights to liberty, equality, justice and the pursuit of happiness are said to be examples of the fundamental rights of humans. In the case of according rights to animals, positions can range from simply giving to animals a minimal moral status through to giving them equality of consideration with humans (where human and animal suffering may count equally). The ultimate Rights position is where the rights of each individual are said to be

---

[5] Jeremy Bentham, Footnote in *Introduction to the Principles of Morals and Legislation*, Chapter 17, 1789

capable of 'trumping' any advantages to others or to society as a whole. This latter position is that of Tom Regan. In *The Animal Rights View* in *Ethical Concerns for Animals*, an RSPCA leaflet of 1990, Regan does not overtly base the accordance of rights upon the ability of animals to suffer, but accords them rights because:

> animals have a life of their own, of importance to them apart from their utility to us. They have a biography, not just a biology. They are not only in the world, they have experience of it. They are somebody, not something. And each has a life that fares better or worse for the one whose life it is.

Because all humans are animals, human rights can be seen as a sub-set of animal rights. To speak constantly of human rights while almost ignoring animal rights is clearly speciesist.

Painist Solutions to the Problems of Aggregation and Rights-Conflicts

The third position is Painism which finds the basis for Regan's ethics to be rather ill-defined. Regan's phrases such as 'a life that fares better or worse' (see above) are perceived as lacking precision. The essence of the issue, I argue, is whether or not an individual suffers pain or distress of any sort, whether cognitive, emotional, sensory or other. Pain, defined broadly in this way, is considered to be the basis of ethics, and unnecessarily causing pain to others (whether animals or aliens or robots) is the essence of evil. (See Chapter 3 *Painism*). The equal consideration of suffering, regardless of species, is a central tenet of this theory. So X amount of pain in a dog or a dodo matters equally with X amount of pain in a human.

Painism, on which I elaborate in the next chapter, combines the Utilitarian emphasis upon pain and pleasure (and happiness) with the Rights Theory emphasis upon the separateness and inviolability of each individual's experience. Importantly, painism can trade-off the pains (sufferings) of one individual against those of another individual but denies absolutely the validity of adding-up the pains (or pleasures) of *several* individuals when calculating right and wrong actions, as is done in Utilitarianism. Painism also offers a solution to one of the principal difficulties in Rights Theory—how to resolve conflicts of rights. In painism this simply becomes a question of preferring whichever right entails the greatest reduction (or avoidance) of individual pain (suffering).

As there is now abundant evidence that animal species are capable of experiencing pain and as Darwinism teaches biological kinship, I believe we should now be practising moral kinship.

Conclusions

We are, after all, all members of the same community of pain. We hear much about the need to encourage a better sense of community. Yet this nearly always, arrogantly, means only a human community. But why stop there? Why not a far wider community—a community of all animals? Or perhaps a community of all mammals? Or at least a community of all apes (including humans)? Sometimes we are told we must respect a feeling of community with all of nature. But this can go too far! What is the point of a community of all creation—what can we genuinely share with distant stars, deadly poisons and diseases? And why a community of all living things—how much can we really be at home with viruses, bacteria and fungal spores? No, the community that really matters morally is this: *the community of all things who can suffer*. Animals are in this sense persons, and so deserve all the respect and rights of personhood. All painient creatures, whether from this planet or any other, really do have a common purpose in our constant struggle against suffering. We are all part of *the great community of pain*. We need to respect each other's sufferings and join in the struggle to help conquer each others' pain, striving everywhere to defeat our common foe. Speciesism is mere bigotry. It is manifestly unfair.

A.C. Grayling has been kind enough to say that the coining of the term 'speciesism' has refocused the debate about the human-animal relationship. Every so often we have to face up to our inconsistencies and irrationalities; facing up to speciesism is such a case.

Attacking speciesism is a challenge to the blind arrogance of the human species. I want to destroy the outrageous narcissism that assumes that human beings are the centre of the universe and that everything else exists merely for our benefit. Copernicus and Gallileo (I am not seriously comparing myself!) encountered some resistance and so did I, especially from those who had something to lose—hunters, farmers and vivisectors. In the 1970s I was even marked down as a dangerous political activist by the British Security Services (M15) who, so I learned later, considered that I or my followers had ulterior political intentions. But I was not seeking to overthrow the state! All I wanted to do was to open the eyes of my selfish species to the sufferings of other animals and to seek to expand the conventional circle of compassion to include them. I sought simply to bring all suffering creation within the bounds of ordinary politics and morality.

As the philosophers Colin McGinn and Peter Singer have rightly pointed out, the argument against the prejudice of speciesism has now been won. It is 'a won argument'. (Foreword). But the consequent revolution in behavior is still to come. New protective laws for animals have been introduced in Europe, America, and even in China, yet we still await the coming of the Golden Age when all suffering animals, together with human animals, are treated with equal respect.

CHAPTER 3
Painism

Introduction

As a psychologist I have always felt that the widespread decline in religion has not so much exposed the god-shaped hole in our human psyche, as a conglomeration of small niches: a niche to reassure us of immortality, a niche for understanding the universe, a niche for trying to influence events and, most importantly, a niche for morality. As I have already argued, our human brains can be so powerful that, when faced with a novel situation, we feel there are a large number of possible alternative ways to react to it. So we need guidance. We need to know how we should behave. This is where morality comes in. Besides, being born with this capacity to be directed by external authority is an essential capacity for any social animal to have.

Dale Jamieson has pointed out that moral theories should be explicit, consistent, universal and valid. Validity, of course, is particularly problematical and there are basically two approaches to it, either by basing our theory upon beliefs that themselves are in no need of justification, or upon other unjustified beliefs. Clearly, neither view is entirely satisfactory. Logical truths that are self-evident (e.g. that all ravens are ravens) do not seem solid enough as foundations for a moral theory. At some point, says Jamieson, justification must end. But where? I believe it ends upon the reality of pain. Surely there is nothing more solidly real than the raw experience of pain itself.

A new secular moral theory is clearly needed for the twenty-first century; one that unifies the confusing hotchpotch of moral fragments that we currently try to live by. We also require a simple language in which to express this theory. This is what the theory of painism tries to provide.

Religion and the Golden Rule

In fact, as we have seen, most religious and secular moralities, although they speak in a dozen different dialects, arrive at a similar conclusion—sometimes called the Golden Rule—that tells us not to do to others what we would not want done to ourselves. Basically, we ought not to cause pain to others, even to those of other tribes and races. This was the moral teaching of the great religions that were developed in the period 900 BC to 700 AD, beginning with Hebrew monotheism and including Daoism and Confucianism in China, Hinduism and Buddhism in India and then continuing on to some of the great Greek philosophers.[1] It was reinforced by Rabbi Hillel and by Jesus and, finally, by Muhammed's commands for practical compassion. Sikhism, Jainism and Zoroastrianism concurred. Compassion, kindness and love are at the core of all the great religions, and were especially in the hearts of their founders. Outstanding among these were the Mahavira (the founder of modern Jainism) and the Buddha, possibly contemporaries in the sixth century BC, not least because these men included all animals within their versions of the Golden Rule.

Why, then, is the world such an unhappy place? In particular, why is so much pain still being caused by human beings to other sensitive individuals, both human and non-human? The answer lies in the duality of human nature. We are psychologically composed not just of natural empathy and love but also of selfishness and greed. The two great forces of good and evil, of compassion and aggression, altruism and selfishness, constantly contend for dominance within us.

---

[1] Karen Armstrong: *The Great Transformation*, Atlantic Books, London, 2006

As I have already claimed, morality has been one of the three great pillars of all religions — the other two being the quests for power and meaning. Religions purported to provide the power to control events — to ensure harvests, for example, and to win wars. They also claimed to provide an explanation of the meaning of the cosmos and of humankind's allegedly special or immortal place within it. These two pillars have been steadily eroded by science. Today science and technology provide far more power than any religion has ever done, and a far deeper and more detailed understanding of the universe. Science, however, does not provide us with a morality — with a framework of ideas as to how we ought to live. That is one of the spiritual vacuums that we face in the twenty-first century.

Secular Moralities

From the days of the ancient Greek philosophers, attempts have been made to formulate a secular morality. It was too easy, and ultimately unconvincing, to argue that morality was the command of the gods. Why, asked the later Humanists, if God was all-powerful and allegedly all-good, was there so much suffering in the world? What was the concrete evidence, anyway, that so-called right and wrong were defined by the wishes of some invisible divinity? The proof was simply lacking.

The Greeks brought reason to bear upon the problem. In modern terms, Aristotle wrote about psychology (how I can be happy) rather than normative ethics (how I should treat others). The Greeks tended to define ethics in terms of personal virtues such as wisdom, moderation, courage, fairness and magnanimity. A second moral language also became established at the time — the language of moral principles such as justice, democracy, equality and liberty. Neither language, however, focused attention onto the suffering of victims. The focus was more abstract and more with the doer than with his victim.

In the nineteenth and twentieth centuries many of the disadvantaged were inspired by the writings of Karl Marx

(1818–1883). But Marx, although moved by the need for class equality, had no clear view of the good society. Indeed, some of his followers actively despised the very concept of morality, seeing it as a device used by the bourgeois to defend their privileges.

The Concept of Rights

It was during the Renaissance in Europe that secular thinkers began to speak more often of the rights of the oppressed and our duties towards them. The viewpoint changed slowly from that of the powerful doer (who was said to display Christian virtues or otherwise) to that of the victim. This tendency grew in the sixteenth century with a demand for individual liberty in matters of belief. Sebastian Castellio, for example, had campaigned for religious toleration against an autocratic church, and was followed by John Milton and John Locke who argued for liberty of expression generally and for rights to life, liberty and property. Towards the end of the seventeenth century the words liberty and right became interchangeable and then, gradually, the latter began to squeeze out the former. The following century saw both the American and French Revolutions— uprisings of the victims (as the revolutionaries saw it) of royal oppression, the former calling for recognition of rights to life, liberty and the pursuit of happiness. The publication of the American Declaration of Independence was in 1776 and in France the Declaration of the Rights of Man and of the Citizen followed in 1789, demanding rights to liberty, property, security and resistance to oppression. With the publication of Thomas Paine's *The Rights of Man* in 1792, the Theory of Rights had become firmly established.

There is still much confusion about the meanings of the word 'rights', and this confusion leads to rather sterile argument. First there is the distinction between moral and legal rights and I propose, for the purposes of this book, to say that a moral right becomes a legal right as soon as it is enshrined in law. This clarifies some of the muddle. Then there are probably four different types of moral rights — the right to do something (a power), the right to receive something (a claim), the right to possess something, and the right to expect something from others. The first three can be called active rights and the last a passive right. Although such distinctions are useful, so much continues to depend upon the overall use of language. Indeed it is often possible to describe the same moral situation in three or four different ways. Take the right to state-protection, for example: I can say that people have a *power* to demand state-protection, or that they can *claim* state-protection, or that they have the *right to possess* state-protection, or the *right to expect* that the state will protect them. In practice the intended results are all much the same. It helps if we face up to the fact that rights are whatever we say they are; they are just human inventions. Indeed, this arbitrariness is one of the worrying aspects of Rights Theory. Can I just arbitrarily conjure up new rights out of thin air? If so, everyone could have a right to a Rolls Royce or a right to be a millionaire! Similarly arbitrary is the concept of duties and, very often, identical moral situations can be described either in rights terminology or in duties language. In the above case, for example, I could say that 'the state has a duty to protect people'. It would save a great deal of heated argument if duty-minded ethicists and rights-minded ethicists tried to understand each others' languages!

Silly confusions of this sort may have been one reason why Jeremy Bentham (1748–1832) rejected the idea of natural rights as being 'nonsense upon stilts'. But he was also against the notion that rights are god-given or exist out there in the universe like stars, planets or other natural phenomena. Bentham was, of course, correct. Rights and duties are defined merely by human thought. Bentham developed the other great secular tradition in British moral thinking — Utilitarianism — which probes deeper into the meaning of what is right and wrong in human action. Bentham concluded that the proper end of action is to achieve *the greatest happiness of the greatest number (including animals)*, and he defined happiness in terms of the intensities and durations of pleasures minus pains. Of course such a felicific calculus was difficult to carry out but it was better, Bentham argued, to deal in facts (such as pain and pleasure) than in lofty fictions such as social contracts or rights. The rightness of an action depends, said Bentham, entirely upon its consequences in terms of the pains and pleasures caused.

Morality is an essential ingredient in politics, and the 1940s saw a revival of political interest in Rights Theory that led to the promulgation of the United Nations Declaration of Human Rights on 10 December 1948. During the 1960s the United Nations added covenants on racial discrimination and further social, civil and political rights. The International Bill of Human Rights currently recognises some forty human legal rights (but none for animals or other nonhumans) ranging from the basic rights to life, liberty and equality of treatment, to more specific rights, such as protections against slavery and torture and rights to food, housing, rest, work, marriage, opinion and privacy. By the middle of the twentieth century, after religious morality had been tested by the horrors of two world wars, three secular moral theories had risen into prominence in the West — Rights Theory, Utilitarianism and Kant's concept of duty. In the 1970s, there was a revival of interest in Utilitarianism, prompted partly by the growing Oxford-based concern for the moral treatment of animals. I published my concerns about speciesism in 1970, seeing it as a form of discrimination similar to racism, ageism, classism and sexism, based as it is upon morally-irrelevant differences between sentient species. Peter Singer's *Animal Liberation* and my own *Victims of Science*, both published in 1975, helped establish the attack upon speciesism and received notable support from Oxford celebrities such as Richard Dawkins, Iris Murdoch and Desmond Morris. I argued for a widening of the moral circle so as to bestow moral concern upon all creatures capable of suffering — not only the other animals of Earth, but sensitive aliens from other worlds and sentient robots, too, if these happened to be encountered. I was also putting the spotlight back onto pain as the one and only evil, defining pain to cover all forms of suffering. Painism became my version of the Golden Rule.

Immanuel Kant

In Germany, however, the tenor of Immanuel Kant (1724–1804) was different. He swung the emphasis away from the victim and back to the moral agent again by arguing that moral action is to be found in purity of intention rather than in its consequences for others. We can calculate what right intention is by applying what Kant calls the Categorical Imperative. This is defined in several ways, one touching upon universality, and another requiring that we should treat persons 'never merely as a means but always also as an end'. Although it is often unclear what Kant means when he writes about ethics, he had the effect in the nineteenth century of reinforcing the importance of the concept of duty. He argued that moral action could be motivated by the power of the will and of reason rather than by spontaneous compassion, or by what David Hume (1711–1776) had described as humanity, sympathy and fellow-feeling. Kant did well to remind us that doing good often goes against our natural selfish impulses. Duties and rights now sometimes found themselves portrayed as rivals, often on the false assumption that only those who can observe duties deserve to have rights. This is clearly wrong, as it would exclude all infants and some invalids, besides animals.

Utilitarianism

Years of pensive analysis brought me to the same conclusion as Jeremy Bentham's—that what really matter in life are pain and pleasure (very broadly defined)—not just as the two great motivators in our lives, but also as the objects of moral action. The psychological truth is that almost everything I do is driven either by the desire to find pleasure or to avoid pain, in an overall quest for happiness. The equally significant moral corollary is that all moral action should increase the pleasures of *others* and reduce their pains so as to enhance their happiness. *Morality is about helping others and not myself.* Like Bentham I feel that happiness (or welfare) is the ultimate objective, but that its basic components—pains and pleasures—are more measurable than happiness itself. As far as I can see, everything that is considered to be good can be described as a pleasure, and all things bad as pains. So all virtues such as magnanimity, moderation and fairness are good simply because they tend to increase the happiness of others. The classical moral principles such as liberty, equality and fraternity are also good only because they usually promote happiness. Rights and duties too are ultimately of moral importance only because they encourage the happiness of others.

How did the founders of Utilitarianism define its moral objectives? Francis Hutcheson (1694–1746) said:

That action is best which procures the greatest happiness for the greatest numbers.[2]

Jeremy Bentham (1748–1832) put it as:

The greatest happiness of the greatest number is the foundation of morals and legislation,[3]

while John Stuart Mill (1806–1873) suggested that:

Actions are right in proportion as they tend to promote happiness, wrong as they tend to promote the reverse of happiness.[4]

So I feel that Utilitarianism, by going straight to the nub of the issue (happiness), is the most pertinent of all the established moral theories. In my view, Bentham's version of Utilitarianism is better than John Stuart Mill's. Mill, rather primly, tried to say that some pleasures (such as those of the intellect, of the feelings and imagination, and of moral sentiments) are of a superior quality to others; thus 'it is better to be a human being dissatisfied than a pig satisfied; better to be Socrates dissatisfied than a fool satisfied'. For Bentham, on the other hand, 'other things being equal, pushpin is as good as poetry'. (Surely somewhere in our nervous systems all pains and pleasures, however superficially different they may appear to be, whether pushpin or poetry, are all rated on the same hedonic scale.) Despite apparently estimating pigs as being less important than Socrates, Mill was

---

[2] Francis Hutcheson: *Treatise II Concerning Moral Good and Evil*, Sec.3,8
[3] Jeremy Bentham: *The Commonplace Book, Works*, x.142, 1789
[4] John Stuart Mill: *Utilitarianism*, London, 1861

not a speciesist and wanted Utilitarianism to embrace the treatment of animals. His harm principle, 'that the only purpose for which power can be rightfully exercised over any member of a civilised community, against his will, is to prevent harm to others', remains the foundation of liberal society.

The Great Flaw in Utilitarianism

Later I became aware of Utilitarianism's central flaw (see pages 75–80). The adding up of the pains and pleasures of different individuals can produce some grotesque results. If painfully experimenting upon a human being, without her consent, for example, creates mild benefits for a million others that add up to more than the victim's pain, then Utilitarianism apparently approves this. (See Peter Singer's Foreword to this volume) Presumably, if the misery of a gang-rape victim is less than the total pleasures of all the rapists, then gang-rape is also a good thing! If the torture of a political prisoner produces comforts for a group of his political adversaries which total more than the prisoner's pain, then some forms of Utilitarianism appear to say that torture is permissible. In other words, Utilitarianism can justify the infliction of agony upon a few in order to provide mere convenience for the many. This has to be wrong.

Rights Theory

The great advantage of Rights Theory is that it protects the individual from the sort of abuses that can be justified by Utilitarianism (see above); it tends to side with the individual victim. In Rights Theory the individual is supreme and the rights of the individual are said to trump all other considerations, such as the greater good or the convenience of many. The experience of each individual is her universe. All our experiences, including pains and pleasures, we experience as individuals and not as groups. No group or nation or species is itself conscious.

The problem with Rights Theory is as follows: it does not focus on what really matters which is, as I have suggested, the experience of happiness. Rights Theorists tend to see each right (e.g. to liberty, freedom of speech, housing, education, religious tolerance etc.) as entirely separate and as ends in themselves. They rarely ask themselves why all these disparate rights are ultimately of value. In consequence there is no way to measure the importance of one right against another. Yet often there are conflicts of rights. If you are suspected of being a dangerous terrorist, for example, can the police just lock you up without a fair trial? Is your right to liberty of less importance than the public's right to safety? How are such conflicts of rights to be resolved?

Lessons to be Learned from Speciesism

As pain (broadly defined) seemed to me to be the essence of evil and as there appeared to be plenty of evidence that humans are not the only species capable of suffering, I could never see why the other animals have been almost invariably left out of the moral picture. (See Chapter 2) Many nonhumans have complex nervous systems, behave like we do when in pain and even have the same neurobiochemicals associated with pain and distress. When I was a schoolboy some of my best friends were animals. Why should their pain matter less than that of the headmaster or the school bully? It seemed to me that if suffering is the central issue in ethics then X amount of pain in Mr Jones should matter exactly the same as X amount of pain in my dog. The vehicle of the pain should be of no distinguishing importance. It is the pain itself that matters morally. I rejected arguments that other animals were not as intelligent as humans or that they lacked immortal souls, or had no autonomy (whatever that meant), or that they could not observe duties. Even if these assertions were true, how could they justify excluding animals from moral concern? All these alleged differences between species were morally irrelevant. The only consideration that mattered morally was whether animals could feel pain and, as far as I could see, science was producing more and more evidence that they could. I was, therefore, very pleased to discover that Jeremy Bentham had reached this same conclusion long before me. I repeat that in 1780 Bentham had said of animals and their treatment – 'The question is not can they reason? Nor, can they talk? But can they *suffer*?' I concurred. It is their capacity to suffer, their painience, that qualifies individuals as moral subjects.

Animal welfare science has made considerable progress. Not only can the *preferences* of animals be tested but so also can their levels of 'pessimism' and 'optimism'. That is to say we can observe their interpretation of ambiguous stimuli as being either pessimistic or optimistic – the 'glass half empty or half full' phenomenon. As such pessimism or optimism is correlated with self-reported happiness in humans we can, by inference, estimate the happiness of animals by the way they interpret ambiguous stimuli. Using such criteria, pigs from enriched environments turn out to be far happier than those from standard commercial accommodation. Such techniques not only help us establish the happiness of animals but can sometimes be an indicator of the happiness of human societies also.

So species membership is no more relevant morally than is the membership of a certain race or class or religion or gender. We have no good grounds for putting the human species in a separate and superior moral category. The huge and ignored moral implication of Darwinism is that, as all animals are related through evolution, we ought to be related morally. Darwin's greatest moral message was that human beings are not unique – our species is but one member of the animal kingdom. We differ from the other species only in degree. Yet, as Darwin himself mused uneasily, we still persist in treating the other animals as our slaves. It is, of course, convenient to do so.

Painism

My own moral theory is called painism and it tries to come to terms with these problems. As regards validity, it recognizes that humans seem naturally endowed with a feeling of compassion for others. We not only recognise the suffering of others, but we innately are driven to do something about it. In particular, we are programmed from birth to develop a recognition of suffering caused by injury, loss of freedom, and by situations of unfairness. Human children, like some of the more intelligent nonhuman animals, are moved instinctively by the perception of such sufferings in others. This is a wonderful thing. On this foundation of natural compassion, therefore, I attempt to build my theory. In this sense, painism goes with the flow of nature. Morality is about how we should treat others, and if we go with our natural compassion, and cultivate it, then altruism can be largely based upon this natural impulse. Moral rules of conduct are then just the icing on the cake. Such rules hold us firm when our baser instincts are in command, preventing our anger, sadism or mere convenience or conformity from overruling our natural compassion and causing pain to others.

Why have I called it *'painism'* when my theory's ultimate moral objective is to increase individual happiness? Well, I could have called it happinessism — but that sounds clumsy. The first step towards happiness is to reduce pain. If pain and pleasure are on one and the same dimension, then I feel that the first thing to do is to deal with the negative (i.e. with pain). Pains are generally psychologically stronger than pleasures and within the same individual will usually dominate. (Unlike pains and pleasures *across* individuals, pains and pleasures *within* the same individual can, for ethical purposes, be added together quite properly.) Besides, pain is more easily measured and identified than is happiness or pleasure; it correlates with certain behaviours and with blood or urine levels of correlated and measurable biochemicals such as cortisol. I have no objection whatsoever to increasing the pleasures of others (we should do this), but in the first place I would prefer to reduce their pains. If happiness becomes more measurable and manageable I would favour placing a greater emphasis upon its increase. Concentrating upon pain may seem to be rather a narrow focus, but I define pain very broadly to cover all forms of suffering ranging from physical agony and clinical depression to degrees of discomfort, distress, boredom, fear, anxiety, guilt, hunger, thirst, cold, dissatisfaction, grief and shame—indeed to include all negative states, whether sensory, cognitive or emotional. To a psychologist, calling all these negative experiences 'pain' can make sense because all are negative reinforcements or aversive stimuli that individuals seek to avoid. So the basic aim of painism is to increase the individual happiness of all suffering creatures by, in the first place, seeking to reduce their individual pains. Painism is about helping others. It is entirely altruistic.

Pains and Pleasures

I think pain and pleasure are, ultimately, on the same 'algesic' scale. Pain is negative while pleasure is positive. Rather as with a thermometer there is a neutral point (like normal body temperature) where the individual feels neither a balance of pain nor of pleasure. Pleasures, however, are harder to measure than pains. They seem to fall into two main categories: those I call *direct* and *indirect*. *Direct pleasures* are such experiences as may arise through the taste of delicious food, the smell of a beautiful perfume, the sound of sweet music; *indirect pleasures* include those caused by the relief of pain. Indirect pleasures are very common and occur, for instance, whenever a painful drive such as hunger or thirst or fear is satisfied or reduced. Most pleasures are in fact combinations of many different pleasures, both direct and indirect, and even the precursors of pleasures (e.g. the thought of impending lunch) can themselves be pleasurable. Because of our natural drive to be compassionate and to care for others, giving pleasure to others, or reducing their pains, may also be a source of pleasure for us. Pains, too, can be divided into *direct* (e.g. a burn, an insult, a loss) and *indirect* (e.g. an unsatisfied drive) The precursors of sensory pains (e.g. worrying about going to the dentist) are also, in themselves, painful, as are the memories of such pains. Psychological terms such as welfare, preference, benefit, reward or reinforcement are, for ethical purposes, all equivalent to pleasure; whereas disadvantage, harm, cost, punishment and negative reinforcement are equivalents to pain. Yet giving pleasure to others—as long as it leads to happiness—remains an important moral issue. The whole of the entertainment world—television, music, the visual arts, literature, theatre and cinema—is about giving pleasure. So is the food industry. Virtually every aspect of our economy is ultimately geared to reducing pain or increasing pleasure and happiness. Those individuals who directly reduce our pains (e.g. nurses, psychotherapists and doctors) are important moral figures. They are the heroes of painism. But how about those who give direct pleasures? They star in the cult of celebrity as actors, comedians and sports people. What, then, of those who purvey pleasure at its most intense—the pornographers and prostitutes? They, too, surely should be considered as heroes and heroines of our moral culture. They have been tainted for far too long by unfair prejudice. Yet it seems too much to ask of everyone that we should constantly be giving pleasure to others. In a totally disinhibited society, especially sexually attractive individuals, for example, would be so occupied by requests for sexual intercourse that they would find it hard to conduct their lives in a way consistent with their own happiness! No, it is more realistic to concentrate upon the relief of pain as our main moral duty. Pain is stronger than pleasure, more measurable and discrete. Let others provide their own direct pleasures while we try to help them with their pains.

What Makes Painism Different:
Not Adding Pains and Pleasures Across Individuals

By emphasising pain (and ultimately happiness) it seems to me that, like Utilitarianism, I am focusing upon what really matters to us all, and not upon rather abstract notions such as rights, virtues or principles. As we have seen, painism avoids the great flaw in Utilitarianism, which is the adding up of the pains and pleasures of separate individuals to make big totals which can lead to absurd cases such as the apparent justification of gang-rape, experiments on unconsenting humans and torture. This is the crucial point on which I have disagreed with Singer since we first met. In Utilitarianism a gang-rape may possibly be deemed to be a good thing if the pleasures of all the rapists, when added together, outweigh the sufferings of the victim. Similarly, a severe experiment on a human (or a small group of humans) may be condoned if it produces a cure for a disease that causes greater total suffering to millions. (See Peter Singer's Foreword.) In Utilitarianism there is the common assumption that the benefits of the many trump the pains of the few.

I have never seen this spelled out but presumably the Utilitarian loosely assumes that the greater the number of those who benefit (e.g. from a painful experiment or political torture or gang rape) the greater is the probability that the *total* of their benefits or pleasures, when added together, will outweigh the totalled pains of the smaller number of victims (of experimentation, torture or rape). Even if the benefits are miniscule in each case, provided there are enough beneficiaries, then this may, of course, be true. But it is nonsense to say that the agony of one individual can be justified because it causes mild comforts to many individuals that happen to be, in total, greater than his agony. *Pains and pleasures have to be experienced to be real, and no-one experiences such totals.* We do not add up the other feelings of a group of people such as their angers, surprises or loves, and expect such totals to be significant, so why do Utilitarians do it with feelings of pain and pleasure?[5] The pains of others are merely the *reports* of pain. Unless our brains were to be connected by futuristic cables that can unify our consciousnesses, I can never say that I directly experience your feelings in addition to mine.

This rejection of the totalling of the pains and pleasures across separate individuals is the most important innovation in painism. It dispenses with the Utilitarian habit of totalling such pains and pleasures and judging actions

---

[5] Richard Ryder: Painism versus Utilitarianism, in *Think*, a Journal of the Royal Institute of Philosophy, Cambridge University Press, Spring 2009, pp. 85–89.

accordingly. Instead, painism rates the goodness or badness of an action by the amount of pain it reduces or causes in the most affected individual. The level of badness of a situation is thus to be measured by the pain of the so-called *maximum sufferer*. A world in which no individual is extremely happy but in which nobody is in extreme pain seems preferable to one in which extremes of pain and unhappiness still exist and are, according to Utilitarianism, justifiable.

Doing away with the adding up (or 'aggregation') of the pains and pleasures of separate individuals does not, however, necessarily invalidate the trading-off of the pains of *one individual* against the benefits to another *individual*. Such cost-benefit analyses *between individuals* are still possible in painism, although a few arbitrary rules have to be adopted.[6] For example, I believe it is always wrong to cause pain to A merely to increase the pleasure of B. But mild pain (such as taxation) may, under certain circumstances, be caused to A in order to reduce the severe pain of B. Torture, of course, is always wrong. In painism cost-benefit analyses, or moral trade-offs as they are sometimes called, can only be between individuals. They are sometimes difficult to calculate. Is it right, for example, to cause pain to a dog in an experiment intended to find a cure, say, for canine distemper? This is not only a question of balancing the intensity and duration of the experimental dog's pain against that of the maximally suffering distemper victim. We have also to take into account questions of certainty or probability. The pain of the experimental dog is almost *certain* to occur, but any benefits from the experiment remain *uncertain*. I conclude that painism should give greater weight to pains and pleasures in proportion to their certainty.

There is another special proviso. If aliens were to offer us the choice between two different types of lives: either (1) a happy childhood followed by a miserable old age or (2) an unhappy childhood and a contented old age, I am sure most

---

[6] Richard Ryder: Painism: Some Moral Rules for the Civilised Experimenter, in *Cambridge Quarterly Healthcare and Ethics*, Cambridge University Press, 1999, pp. 8, 36–43

people would opt for the latter, even if the sufferings of their childhoods (in (2)) exceeded considerably those of old age in the first option (1). In other words 'all's well that ends well'. Later pains weigh a great deal more than earlier ones.

Many have regretted the increasing individualism of modern society. Why has it happened? The obvious reason is that we all need others far less than we did. We are no longer reliant upon other individuals for our safety, food and support. Instead we have the welfare state. As individuals we pay our taxes and, when the time comes, we draw on our investment in the form of education for our children, benefits, pensions, protection and a free health service. Women, like men, can now work and have careers and do not need husbands to look after them. Besides, *it is the individual and not the group who actually feels and experience pain, distress and happiness*.

Of course, each individual still needs contact with other individuals. No man is an island unto himself. Except, perhaps, in the case of some autistic people, but even then some contact with others appears to be desirable. What do we need others for? We obviously need adults in childhood to look after us, but less so as we become adult ourselves, until we are old or infirm. Provided we have an income we can buy food and shelter for ourselves in most modern societies. Admittedly, we may need others for sexual contact, love, friendship and approval. We like to be liked and, for some people, their self-esteem is dependent upon the esteem of others.

One of the important tenets of painism is that we should concentrate upon the individual because it is the individual —not the race, the nation nor the species—who does the actual suffering. For this reason, the pains and pleasures of several individuals cannot meaningfully be totalled, as occurs in Utilitarianism and some other moral theories. We have seen that one of the problems with the Utilitarian view is that, for example, the sufferings of a gang-rape victim can, absurdly, be justified if the rape gives a greater sum total of pleasure to the rapists! But consciousness, surely, is bounded by the boundaries of the individual. As I have already said, my pain and the pain of others are thus in separate categories; you cannot add or subtract them from each other. They are worlds apart. Without directly experiencing pains and pleasures they are not really there — we are counting merely their husks. Unless it is experienced, pain is not pain. Thus, for instance, inflicting 100 units of pain on one individual is, I would argue, far worse than inflicting a single unit of pain on a thousand or a million individuals, even though the so-called 'totals' of pain in the latter cases are far greater. In any situation we should thus concern ourselves initially with the pain of the individual who is the maximum sufferer. It does not matter, morally speaking, who or what the maximum sufferer is — whether human, nonhuman or machine. Pain is pain regardless of who experiences it.

The realisation that costs and benefits (or pains and pleasures) *cannot be totalled across individuals* invalidates not only Utilitarianism but aspects of democracy also. Majorities lose their magic. Total votes no longer matter. The idea that causing agony to one or two individuals is alright if it benefits 'the public' at large, or some other huge majority, is simply false. It is especially false if the pains of the few are intense while the benefits to the many are trivial.

In his foreword to this book, Peter Singer, who is defending the Utilitarian position against Painism, asks: 'What are we to do if the only way to prevent pain to many is to inflict pain on one?' Painism answers that it is certainly not right to inflict agony on one individual just in order to prevent the slight sufferings of many. However, painism may allow the infliction of pain on one in order to prevent the far greater pain of another *individual*. In conclusion, there are at least four, admittedly arbitrary, qualifications I have added:

- It is always wrong to increase someone's *pain* merely in order to increase the *pleasure* of others
- Where pain (or pleasure) is *certain* then it counts for far more than when it *uncertain*. (The pain of a severe experiment, for example, is pretty certain whereas its proposed benefits are in the future and so are usually uncertain.)

- A prohibition is placed upon the infliction of any pain that is *severe* or *long lasting* (e.g. in the case of torture).
- *Later pains trump earlier pains.* So it is better to have an unhappy childhood and die painlessly rather than the other way around.

What painism avoids is tyranny by the majority: the half-spoken assumption that the interests of the *many* automatically trump the interests of the *few* (or one). Majorities do not matter morally; all that matters is the intensity and duration of each individual's pain.

Grading Pain

Pains and pleasures are usually calculated on the two dimensions of *intensity* and *duration*, and this is convincing but only up to a point. Which is the most desirable life to lead—one that begins with fifty years of misery and ends with twenty years of happiness, or one that starts with fifty years of happiness and ends with twenty years of misery? Clearly, the latter has, in total, the most happiness. But it ends badly. Does the chronological order of our hedonic experiences matter? Is it ultimately more desirable to lead a life that ends well than one that is mostly full of contentment? The present seems to trump the past. Later events and experiences seem to count for more than do earlier ones.

Pain can more easily be measured than pleasure, and animal welfare scientists have led the way in doing so. When I was campaigning in the 1970s for new British legislation to protect laboratory animals, and trying to include some standard measures of suffering, the argument I encountered was that suffering could *not* be measured—at least not by those officials who would be charged with the administration of any new law (eventually the Animals (Scientific Procedures) Act of 1986). But I knew that certain objective measures of stress were already available: cortisol levels in the blood, for example, and levels of blood pressure, heart rate and skin conductivity. Stress, however, is a tricky concept as it does not correlate entirely with suffering. Not only pains but intense pleasures can also increase stress. Stress is more a measure of overall arousal, and the physiological indicators of intense pleasure and pain are remarkably similar. It was this lack of objective physiological distinguishers between pain and pleasure that was irksome. Even on the behavioural level species-differences could be deceptive. When in pain some species become active while others (those wired to avoid predators not by flight but by hiding) lie still. Generally, of course, most mammals react to pain by writhing, vocalising and attempts to escape or avoid the source of their pain or fear. I was also accustomed to judging the varying depths of clinical depression in my patients and there were, generally, reasonably high correlations on the rating of severity of depression both among diagnosticians, and between the diagnosticians and the depressed patients themselves. All this was encouraging as we fought for a new law to protect animals from pain and distress in research. I continued to urge that measurements be made along the two dimensions of the *intensity* and *duration* of suffering in *individual* (not average) animals. Eventually, in 1986, the new Act was passed and the civil service in London gradually established the habit of regularly assessing various levels of animal suffering (pain and distress) in the experimental procedures they were licensing. Eventually the EU sought to catch up with the UK in this regard and set up an expert working group in 2008 in connection with the revision of the EU's own Directive (86/609/EEC) on the protection of animals used for scientific purposes. In 2009 this working group recommended that scientific procedures on animals should be banded into four severity categories according to the 'degree of pain, suffering, distress or lasting harm' expected, or actually experienced, by any individual animal. These four categories are:

- **Non-recovery:**
  Procedures, which are performed entirely under general anaesthesia from which the animal shall not recover consciousness.

- **Mild:**
  Procedures on animals as a result of which the animals are likely to experience short term mild pain, suffering or distress. Procedures with no significant impairment of the wellbeing or general condition of the animals.

- **Moderate:**
  Procedures on animals as a result of which the animals are likely to experience short term moderate pain, suffering or distress, or long-lasting mild pain, suffering or distress. Procedures that are likely to cause moderate impairment of the wellbeing or general condition of the animals.

- **Severe:**
  Procedures on animals as a result of which the animals are likely to experience severe pain, suffering or distress, or long-lasting moderate pain, suffering or distress. Procedures that are likely to cause severe impairment of the wellbeing or general condition of the animals.

I would suggest that these sort of definitions can also be applied to ordinary life events in human as well as nonhuman animals, where, for example, we seek to prohibit entirely the infliction of severe suffering on moral grounds, or perhaps permit mild suffering in certain cost-benefit situations (between individuals). Note the adjudged equivalence of 'long lasting moderate' pain with 'severe' pain, and 'moderate' pain with 'long lasting mild' pain etc. This is a new and important principle in governance.

Painism and Rights Theory

Of course, as I have already said, preferences and tastes differ between species and individuals so we need not always demand exact equality of treatment. Individuals react differently to the same stimulus. Thus we do not have to accord dogs freedom of religion, for example — it is not something they derive much joy from! We should expect, however, equal respect to be given when it comes to pains and pleasures. So if a dog gets the same amount of pleasure from chewing a bone as a devotee derives from observing

TABLE THREE

	Rights Theory	Utilitarianism	Painism
Totalling of pains and pleasures <u>across</u> individuals is allowed	n.a.	√	X
Pains and pleasures (happiness) are of paramount importance	X	√	√
Trade-offs of pains and pleasures <u>between</u> individuals are allowed	n.a.	√	√ But between single individuals only

A Comparison between the three Ethical Theories

her (harmless) religion then both the religion and the bone, in each case, should be equally promoted!

How, then, does painism impinge upon Rights Theory? The two theories share the advantage of respecting absolutely the importance of the individual. In painism's case this is because it recognises that the boundaries of consciousness (and in particular of pain, pleasure and happiness) are the boundaries of the individual. So like Rights Theory, painism puts a protective fence around the individual. Ultimately, the most important right is the right of each individual not to be caused unwanted pain.

Painism can, however, help with the problems of Rights Theory and deal with any difficulties that arise when two or more rights are in conflict. Pains and pleasures, unlike rights, are very real. They lack any arbitrariness and, being on the same dimension, when in conflict they can (theoretically at least) be measured one against another. All rights are in fact concerned with preventing or reducing pains (or increasing pleasures and happiness) and so, if these hedonic values are calculated, conflicts of rights can be resolved in this manner. For example, there are sometimes conflicts between the right to protest politically and the right to be protected from the nuisance caused by such political protests. So if a noisy political protest meeting will cause 5 units of pain to the most upset innocent neighbour, and the suppression of the protest meeting causes only 4 units of pain to the maximally upset protestor, then the police are morally justified in suppressing the meeting. To resolve a conflict of rights one must first estimate the pain-reducing value of each right, and then give preference to the greater.

Negative Utilitarianism

Painism is not the same as Negative Utilitarianism. *The latter theory still adds up sufferings across separate individuals*. It claims that the best actions are ones that produce the least *overall* amount of unhappiness added up across all the individuals affected by an action. Negative Utilitarianism is also vulnerable to the criticism that the best way to eliminate all suffering in the world would be to kill humanely all painient beings. Apart from the practical difficulties in ensuring that all deaths would be painless and unfeared, the problem here is that millions of perennially happy individuals would also die. Painism, however, treats each individual individually and so is a far more discriminating and precise instrument than is Negative Utilitarianism.

Measuring Rights

A huge variety of alleged human rights, and some fewer animal rights, have been claimed over the last century, and are now listed in various legal conventions.

The United Nation's *Universal Declaration of Human Rights* (1948) was later divided in 1966 into *Civil and Political Rights* on one hand and *Economic, Social and Cultural Rights* on the other. Among others the following rights were listed: to life, liberty and security, the freedom of movement, rights to rest, leisure, holidays, education, equal pay, to work, to favourable conditions of work, to security in unemployment, sickness and disability, old age and widowhood, rights to assistance in motherhood and childhood, to an adequate standard of living, food, clothing, housing, medical care, freedom of thought, conscience and religion, equality before the law, not to be tortured and not to be enslaved. But is it possible to put all these quite different rights on to the same dimension? Is it possible to rank order the above list of rights? Most writers and jurists have found this difficult. Yet surely it is possible, at least theoretically, because all these rights are morally important only in as much as they reduce pain (suffering). So all have their 'hedonic' values. Thus, if there is a conflict between, say, the right not to be tortured and the right to be clothed, the intensity and duration of the pain associated with each condition needs to be estimated and compared. In most cases the quantity of individual pain associated with torture will far exceed that of being inadequately clothed, so if there is a conflict between the two rights it is not difficult to see which should have priority. Each case will, of course, be different, depending upon individual circumstances including the sensitivities of different victims. But, once rights are reduced to their essential hedonic values (i.e. how much pain they reduce or pleasure they cause) there is no difficulty in principle in ranking them and then giving priority to whichever comes first.

The Implications of Painism

Too often in everyday life we concern ourselves with numbers of sufferers. We ask how many people died in a battle? How many suffered in a famine? How many were injured in a bomb outrage? Was one atrocity morally worse than another because it had more victims? Painism says such numbers are irrelevant because the sufferings of separate individuals cannot meaningfully be totalled. Instead, painism concentrates upon the levels of individual sufferings (their intensities and durations), and rates the badness of a situation by the individual who suffers most i.e. the maximum sufferer. So the badness of an action is measured not by how many suffered, but by how much pain was felt by the most affected victim.

Which is most important morally-speaking: improving the mere comfort of ten individuals or reducing the agony of one? Painism sides with the individual in agony. Actual moral dilemmas of this sort occur in casualty departments, on battle fields and in welfare charities. Whom should I help first? Other factors such as treatability being equal, painism's answer is that I should first help those in greatest pain. (Unconscious wounded are still important because of the pain they may feel on recovery and because of the pain their friends and relatives will feel if they die or remain untreated.) The infliction of involuntary and unnecessary pain is quite simply wrong wherever it occurs. Pain is a fact, a very powerful fact, and not a fiction. You can argue about the reality and rightness of abstracts such as virtues, principles and social contracts, but you cannot argue about the reality of pain!

What about the taking of life? Does painism respect the right to life? Suppose I decide to kill a wild animal instantaneously and without causing it any suffering, is that wrong? Surely, if my action does not cause suffering, even to third parties, it cannot be wrong. If I did the same to a human, however, I would inevitably cause grief to my victim's friends and fear to others who might worry that they could be the next to be murdered. So killing a human — or any animal where the humane slaughter provokes fear or sadness in others — is always likely to be wrong. I do not accept the hoary old argument that killing is wrong because it terminates 'the valuable opportunities that continued life would afford' because once dead, we assume, we are aware of nothing so there is no awareness of missed opportunities. There is, simply, no more suffering. Indeed, by killing we are also liberating our victims from the likelihood of further pain.

Painism is concerned entirely with an action's *consequences* for the victim. But 'actions' covers both *commissions* and *omissions*. Because of its total commitment to consequences, *painism treats omissions and commissions equally*. Scan-studies have found that we naturally tend to attach more emotional importance to commissions than to omissions, even where their consequences for the victims are the same. Commissions seemingly provoke more 'blame' than do omissions. This irrational imbalance needs to be rectified in practice.

It can be seen that painism has some considerable consequences for democracy. Democracy is based upon approximate Utilitarian principles, giving preference to the wishes and welfare of majorities over the welfare of minorities and individuals. This has been dubbed 'a tyranny by the majority'. Clearly, minorities and individuals also need protection. Human rights have been introduced as a device to provide such welcome protection. So we have in most democracies an incompatible mixture of two imperfect moral theories, Utilitarianism and Rights Theory, cobbled together out of expediency. By using painism instead we could have one unified moral theory.

Applied painism would, of course, also bring into the moral, social and political community all painient beings regardless of their species. The boundaries of the moral and political community are not limited by the boundaries of species but by the boundaries of painience. All animals are part of this community of pain. As painism focuses upon the pain, pleasure and happiness of the individual regardless of their race, gender or species, nonhuman animals should always, as a matter of routine and of public policy, be brought into the moral calculations of private and political life. X amount of pain in a pig matters equally with X amount of pain in Socrates!

Painism is concerned with actual suffering and so focuses upon the present and the future rather than the past. It concerns itself with errors of omission as well as those of commission, because it matters not to a victim whether her pain is caused by deliberate cruelty or by neglect; the motives of the moral agent are irrelevant to the sufferer. So painism is a victim-centred morality that is hardly concerned with the virtues, principles or righteousness of the moral agent. It focuses on pain and distress wherever these occur. Painism is the antithesis of selfishness and meets the requirements for universality, consistency and explicitness. Its implications are certainly radical. The waging of war, for example, because it is almost certain to cause severe individual suffering, is hardly ever justifiable under painism except, perhaps, in defence, and as a last resort. Above all, painism is concerned with the quantity of individual suffering and not with the number of sufferers. Painism is about helping others; it asserts the utter importance of each and every individual sufferer. Painism may seem counter-intuitive to some, and particularly to those who have become habituated to using the *numbers of sufferers* rather than the *quantity of individual suffering*, as the measure of social wrongs. But I believe painism is a more valid and a more rational system than either Utilitarianism or Rights Theory, and can serve to unite the strengths of both, thereby providing a truer and more consistent secular moral theory for the twenty-first century.

CHAPTER 4
Happiness For Others

I have argued for a radical change in moral outlook. My first proposal is that all animals should be included within the moral circle. Indeed, any individual capable of feeling pain or distress of any sort should be part of the moral community and have moral standing. This includes any sensitive robots or aliens we may encounter in the future. The sufferings of all such painient beings deserve equal respect. Equal pain requires equal treatment, regardless of race, sex or species. Speciesism is to be rejected. (Chapter 2)

The second radical change I am proposing is the theory of painism itself. (Chapter 3) This moral theory tries to bring together the good points of Rights Theory (chiefly, a respect for the individual) with the strengths of Utilitarianism (the quest for happiness through reduced pains and increased pleasures). Painism also provides solutions to some of the main difficulties with these theories — for example the gang rape and torture problems of Utilitarianism and the problem encountered in Rights Theory when rights conflict. I have expounded, rationally I hope, my moral theory of painism. Incidentally, I call it *painism* rather than *sentientism* because I am wanting to focus upon pain (and unhappiness) rather than on the full range of sensations. Initially, in the 1980s, I *did* sometimes refer to it as sentientism in order to emphasise my concern with all sensate or conscious beings. But, theoretically at least, this could include aliens from another planet who are highly conscious but cannot feel any pain at all! (Their warning system to help them avoid dangers would, presumably, be merely like a flashing red light — with no feelings attached to it.) So, in order to avoid such difficulties, from about 1990, I have used the term *painism* to describe a theory that could be used to alter and consolidate our whole moral (and political) outlook.

When faced with a moral dilemma I believe we have to ask ourselves the question—which individuals (regardless of species) are likely to suffer the greatest pain?' When we have answered that we are well on the way to knowing what we should be doing about it. The maximum sufferers should be our first concern. We have to remember that when facing all moral issues we should perform three basic tasks:

- find the suffering
- reduce the suffering of the maximum sufferers
- then reduce all suffering as far as possible

Selfishness is a terrible thing. It is the antithesis of morality. Yet we seem to live in an increasingly selfish society. People are not being educated to think of the happiness of others. The great goodness of the Christian (and other) religions was to teach a concern for others—for the poor and needy in particular. This is what Christian love for neighbours was all about. In Britain the church is no longer there in the lives of most people and this has left a burgeoning selfishness. Thousands just think of their own personal interests and to hell with those of strangers, colleagues or even spouses. We have seen the growing poison of selfishness both in the work place (for example in banking) and in private life. The new dependency culture breeds a type of person who expects everything for nothing. Painism could be an antidote to this poison by stressing the importance of *others*—of every other individual who can feel pain.

In this final chapter I will consider how painism deals with some current moral issues, the position of the individual, the failings of democracy, fairness, tyranny by the majority, the possible future development of moral government and the chief causes of happiness.

What Causes Happiness?

What, then, are the true sources of happiness? Research shows that people desire secure jobs, health and feelings of love and achievement. They want to have friends they can trust. When it comes to material goods they want sufficient money so as not to worry, a decent level of comfort, and to be able to compare themselves favourably with the material conditions enjoyed by others. This last point seems to correlate with the traditional principle of equality; our envy of those who are (unequally) better off than ourselves is a major source of unhappiness.

When asked to rate the 'wellbeing' they felt in various situations, a group of American women rated their top seven activities as:

1) sex
2) socialising
3) relaxing
4) praying/worshipping/meditating
5) eating
6) exercising
7) watching television

A survey presented by Michael Mosely for the BBC in 2011 found that members of the British public rated their top pleasures in the following order:

1) family and friends
2) sex
3) food

The greatest pain was said to be the *loss of loved ones* through death, rejection or other means.[1]

---

[1] Michael Moseley and Victoria Bell: *Pleasure and Pain with Michael Moseley*, BBC 1, 25 January 2011

Happiness, Pleasure and Pain

What, then, are the relationships between happiness and pleasure? Happiness has been defined in various ways and distinguished from pleasure usually on two grounds. First, happiness is more than merely sensory. One does not usually talk of happiness in the experience of a good meal, a hot bath, a fine whisky or a visit to the opera. These experiences can be pleasures but not happinesses. Yet we all recognise that having experienced these things we are subsequently more likely to be happy. Secondly, happiness endures whereas pleasures are fleeting. *So happiness is a more comprehensive state than is pleasure and tends to last far longer.* We talk of happy marriages, happy careers and happy lives. In other words happiness is similar to pleasure but tends to pervade the whole person and to endure.

Brain Correlates of Happiness

Biochemical changes in the brain, such as abnormal levels of the neurotransmitters serotonin and dopamine, are found to be associated with mania and depression. Dopamine, in particular, is now generally accepted as also being associated with love, exhilaration, joy, elation and happiness.[2] Current thinking tends to correlate raised levels of certain neuro-chemicals with various mental states as follows:

- Romantic love and parenthood — oxytocin
- Wants and desires — dopamine
- Euphoria — internal opioids

Sexual arousal leads to increased levels of both dopamine and internal opioids. After orgasm there are also raised levels of serotonin.

The neurophysiology of happiness is beginning to be better understood and MRI scans have begun to identify systems within the brain which are associated with both happiness and pleasure. Objective studies have tended to confirm that:

---

[2] G S Krantz et al: Reward and the Serotonergic System, *Neuroscience* 166, 4, April 2010

- pain and pleasure involve some of the same neurophysiological circuits
- some circuits are activated by *all* varieties of pleasure, regardless of content
- pleasures are indeed positively correlated with happiness
- variety or novelty sustains pleasures[3]

So it begins to become acceptable to see pleasures as indeed being components of happiness. Pleasures are fleeting experiences and always have an object, whereas happiness is a more general, lasting and diffuse experience. The 'wanting' or desiring part of a pleasure (which itself is sometimes experienced as a mixture of both pain and pleasure) seems to be associated with *dopamine* in the brain whereas the 'liking' part of a pleasure may be associated also with *serotonin* - one of the main neurotransmitters associated with mood. Once again we note the possible positive connections between happiness and mood, and between happiness and pleasure.

It has been found that feelings of joy and compassion are associated with activity in the *left prefrontal cortex* whereas feelings of depression and pessimism are correlated with activity in the *right prefrontal cortex* (in right-handed subjects).[4] Meditation of the variety recommended by Buddhists as a promoter of happiness has been shown to produce high frequency gamma brainwaves (EEG), especially in the left hemisphere. (See pp 97–100)

The Big Seven Causes of Happiness

If we are going to formulate an ethics based upon causing happiness to others then we need to study how to do this. In the twentieth century a whole literary industry grew up

---

[3] A C Grayling: *Exchanges at the Frontier*, BBC Radio 4, 25 November 2010

[4] R J Davidson and M Rickman: Behavioural Inhibition and the Emotional Circuitry of the Brain, in L A Schmidt and J Schulkin, eds: *Extreme Fear and Shyness : Origins and Outcomes*, Oxford University Press, Oxford and New York, 1999

purporting to provide techniques for achieving happiness, and many such popular solutions may have efficacy. The distinguished economist Richard Layard summarised the science of the subject in his important *Happiness : Lessons from a New Science* in 2004, pinpointing *the 'Big Seven'* main factors that have been shown to affect levels of happiness in human societies. These are:

- family relationships (measured crudely by divorce rates)
- financial security
- work (measured, for example, by employment levels)
- community and friends (for example, level of trust of others and membership of non-religious bodies)
- health
- personal freedom (for example, due to quality of government)
- personal values (for example, a belief in god or in a morality)

In brackets I have added some factors which seem to be related and which emerge in other cross-cultural studies as being of significance.

The first five of the above factors are given in their apparent order of importance. Some massive international surveys have supported these results.[5] It is well established that *personal and family friendships* are of paramount importance and part of the value of *work* is also as a source of such friendships.[6] These findings tend to vindicate Sigmund Freud's observation made a hundred years earlier that the two great secrets of happiness are to *be able to love and to work*. Friendship has been highly regarded as a cause of happiness since at least the days of Epicurus, and feeling able to trust others has been shown to be an important part of this.

---

[5] Layard, Richard: *Happiness: Lessons from a New Science*, Penguin Books, London, 2006
[6] Michael Argyle: *The Psychology of Happiness*, Methuen, London 1987

The other psychological component of *work* that relates strongly to happiness appears to be *self-esteem*: feeling that one is good at the job. *Unemployment*, not just because of its consequent poverty, is a potent source of misery in itself because of the loss of such self-esteem. The unemployed person often feels a lack of achievement and so a lack of personal value. They feel that they are not admired or needed by others for what they can do.

The *quality of work* also matters. Since Hegel the concept of *alienation* has been used to describe the malaise of the worker who feels no sense of satisfaction or self-fulfilment at his job and no connection with the product. So work can be a powerful source of both self-identity and self-esteem. But, to an extent, these effects are dependent upon the culture of the so-called 'Protestant work ethic' which highly values work. In the twenty-first century some of those unemployed who are dependent on the state get accustomed to unemployment and a new *culture of dependency* develops. Although this may create serious problems for a state's economy it can be a novel source of happiness for some individuals. Some seem content to live off the state (i.e. off taxpayers), just as many women grew accustomed to being dependent on their husbands in earlier years.

Perhaps because it has some psychological truth in it, *alienation* is one of the few Marxist concepts to have survived the passage of time. Marx may well have been right to describe the alienation of factory workers in the mills of the industrial revolution. Rarely did they feel satisfaction or fulfilment in the jobs they did. They felt little connection with their products and gained scant praise or social esteem for their work. Ironically, communism itself, as it in fact manifested in the twentieth century, produced massive alienation not only at work but in everyday existence. Communism certainly did not produce happiness. Many who lived in a communist state have testified to this and to their intense sense of a denial of personal freedom.

Having *friends* has traditionally been associated with happiness. But it is uncertain whether friends create happiness or happiness creates friends. A happy person is fun to be with whereas a depressed person very often is not. Buddhists often stress that giving love and compassion towards others is its own reward, as it leads to happiness in the giver of the love. It is interesting that brain studies reveal that happiness and showing compassion to others are both associated with raised levels of dopamine.

A sense of *personal freedom* depends to a large extent upon the culture and the quality of the government of a society and Layard has listed six relevant features of good government:

- the rule of law (justice)
- voice and accountability (democracy and the freedom of speech)
- absence of corruption (honesty)
- efficiency of regulation
- effectiveness of government services (for example the welfare state)
- stability and lack of violence (peace and security)

Again I have entered in brackets some traditional principles or conditions which appear to be correlated. We can see that the idea that these old principles such as liberty, justice, equality, peace and democracy are *stepping stones* to happiness appears to be supported by these modern findings. (The above six features of good governance are, for example, what the United Nations should be trying to promote in Iraq, Afghanistan and worldwide, through training and aid.)

There is certainly evidence that *religious beliefs tend to enhance happiness*. This seems to me to be due to three types of effect:

- The first is the *content* of such beliefs. Being convinced, for example, that one will have an afterlife in heaven can, understandably, make one happier, (Content can, also, of course, have the opposite effect making one miserable as, for example, with the belief that one is damned and destined for hell-fire.)

- The second type of effect is *functional* where the actual process itself of prayer (meditation), regular ritual or cognitive structure (meaning) all seem to be soothing.
- Finally, there are the *accidental spin-offs* of being religious such as the socialising at places of worship, the singing of hymns and the performing of family get-togethers. All these can also increase happiness.

Religion, however, is a risky technique for enhancing happiness. It can work but, like a drug, it can also have bad side-effects when guilt or sectarian differences or fanaticism take over. Furthermore, like a pain-killing drug, religion can indeed become addictive.

The Control of Happiness

To what extent then is happiness innate (genetic) and to what extent is it caused by events in our lives? A popular view is that genetics determines approximately 50 per cent of our happiness, while 40 per cent is determined by the way we perceive and think about our lives, and 10 per cent is caused by our circumstances.[7] Some Buddhists might not be content with this allocation and would want to claim that up to 100 per cent of our happiness *can, with proper training*, be under our own control. There are, however, two slightly different questions here:

- what proportion of our happiness is determined by innate (genetic) factors?
- how far can we learn to override these genetic (and other) causes of happiness/unhappiness?

It is worth noting that the distinction between genetic and other causes does not imply that only the non-genetic causes are susceptible to change through the application of skills. It is now known that the repetition of mental and physical behaviours can alter the physiology of the brain. How about beliefs, values and expectations? Do these affect happiness? Buddhists, positive thinkers, Yogins and cogni-

---

[7] Aaron Jarden and Dan Weijers: *Wipe that Smile off your Face*, The Philosopher's Magazine, 1st quarter 2011, pp. 53–59

tive therapists might all assert that they do.[8] Having some sort of value system (as opposed to none) does appear to work, as do certain optimistic beliefs (such as the belief in personal immortality). Everyday expectations that are too high, however, can be the source of much unhappiness when disillusionment sets in. Yet there remains a chicken and egg situation here. To what extent are beliefs and values themselves the products of mood? Which comes first? Very often it is the mood that promotes the belief and not the other way around. In any case, severe depression will entirely dominate such cognitive states and depressives are not often able to pull themselves together, nor 'believe' themselves into a state of happiness.

As I have said, I believe religion has three main psychological functions which I have called *meaning, magic* and *morality*. All three tend to produce happiness. Providing believers with answers (however untrue) to the great imponderables such as the origin of the universe, the meaning of life and the assurance of immortality, reduces our otherwise constant state of uncertainty about these issues. Believing that prayer to an omnipotent god will produce helpful results in our everyday struggles, likewise tends to reduce our levels of anxiety. Thirdly, having a clear-cut prescription as to what is good behaviour also reduces our worries about which actions we should choose to take.

The Buddhist Approach to Controlling Happiness

Buddhism sees unhappiness as the *reaction* to natural suffering. That is to say it is within our powers to be happy or unhappy depending upon the deployment of certain mental skills which we can learn. As we have seen, happiness is more generalized than pleasure and more long-lasting. Unlike pleasure, so Buddhists say, true happiness is never linked with negative states such as cruelty, pride, greed or violence. So pleasure and happiness are distinct. Happiness is also, according to Buddhists, distinct from euphoria.

---

[8] H.H. Dalai Lama and Howard C. Cutler: *The Art of Happiness*, Hodder & Stoughton, 1998

Above all, Buddhism views unhappiness as the way we experience life's usual sufferings. As Matthieu Ricard puts it: 'the mind translates suffering into unhappiness.[9]

Suffering is, say the Buddhists, universal, but everyone has the capacity to reduce it. Buddha's Four Noble Truths are that:

1) there is suffering everywhere
2) the causes of suffering are negative feelings such as desire, attachment, malice, pride and anger, but such mental poisons can be eliminated so that
3) an end to suffering is therefore possible
4) by following the path i.e. by using certain skills

What, then, are these suffering-reducing skills? There are three main techniques says Ricard:

- using mental imagery
- awakening ourselves to love and compassion
- developing our inner strength

Mental Imagery

When afflicted with pain we should visualize something beautiful. Ricard says 'we can visualize, for instance, a soothing, luminous nectar that soaks into the centre of the pain and gradually dissolves it into a feeling of wellbeing.'

Awakening Ourselves to Love and Compassion

We need to remember that others are far worse afflicted than we are. As we offer compassion and loving kindness to others our pain does not feel so oppressive.

Developing Inner Strength

By practising meditation on inner peace and compassion. Ricard describes four forms of such meditation:

- cultivating an 'all pervading sense of benevolence' so that ' love and compassion permeate our entire mind'. We

---

[9] Matthieu Ricard: *Happiness: A Guide to Developing Life's Most Important Skill*, Atlantic Books, p 247, 2003

generate a total readiness and unconditional availability to benefit others.

- focusing attention and concentration upon a chosen object and calling back one's mind each time it wanders 'in a clear, calm and stable' manner.

- cultivating 'a clear, open, vast and alert state of mind, free from mental constructs'. This 'open presence' is not focused on anything particular, yet it is not distracted. 'The mind simply remains at ease, perfectly present in a state of pure awareness.' Intruding thoughts are 'allowed to vanish naturally'.

- Visualising a complex mental image such as a representation of a Buddhist figure - imagining every detail of the face, clothes and posture and 'inspecting them one by one'.

Richard Davidson and others have found that meditators who are practiced in these skills show high levels of brain activity called gamma waves and, on MRI scanning, raised levels of left prefrontal activity.[10]

Thoughts on the Big Seven

At a time when some of the 'Big Seven' happiness-promoters have been booming in the West (e.g. incomes, personal freedom, employment and health) one may ask why average happiness in the year 2000 was no greater than in the year 1950. The answer may be that some of the other happiness-promoters (e.g. family and communal relationships, and personal values) have declined. Judging by divorce rates and membership figures for communal organisation these declines are real. The decline in personal values—which includes a belief in morality—seems to be especially germane to this book. Studies suggest that on average we feel less certainty about what is right and wrong than we used to. In the West our moral code was based upon a Judaeo-Christian model that was widely challenged in the

---

[10] R J Davidson, J Kabat-Zinn e al: Alterations in Brain and Immuno Function produced by Mindfulness Meditation, *Psychosomatic Medicine*, 65, 2003, pp 564–70

decades following World War II and has not yet been replaced. Secular society, and even Christianity itself, have been moving through a period of moral change. Now may be the time to recreate a moral code taking into account advances in science, as well as crucial social changes such as higher educational standards, better incomes, new technologies, contraception and the advent of welfare states around the globe. Having a clear morality itself can increase happiness. Sadly, that branch of psychology which has tried to address the subject of happiness has produced results that are merely banal. It may be unsurprising that a field based upon some appallingly cruel research on animals should have failed to become more edifying. So far this approach has only stated the obvious. Its emphasis on training techniques is nothing original and has been chiefly a question of providing new names for old tricks.

As Layard has pointed out, more and more people in the West are now divorced, separated or never married and this appears to lower average levels of happiness. (Marriage averagely adds seven years to the life of a man and four to that of a woman). Levels of trust, too, have fallen in some countries. But greater democracy and participation in government have usually increased happiness. In a comparative study across Swiss Cantons, for example, those with greater rights to determine government policy through referenda were found to be far happier than those allowed less power.

Layard spotlights the spread of television, the change in gender roles and growing individualism as factors affecting happiness. The introduction of television initially had the effect of reducing communal activities as people stayed at home to watch the screen. The content of television as well as that of the other media, has become increasingly trivial, violent and sexual. Soap operas have made it seem that other people's ordinary lives are chaotic and hysterical, full of emotion and drama. Actors are often selected for their good looks and the cult of celebrity has made viewers feel that other people are not only wealthier than they are, but also far more beautiful. Envy (inequality), as we have seen, is the source of much unhappiness. On the other hand, studies have shown that television can also genuinely be a source of much happiness, especially for the old and lonely. So television has created a mixed response, making some happy yet, at the same time, creating envy by exaggerating the wealth and beauty of others.

Happiness studies by Layard, Andrew Oswald and others have relied heavily upon self-reports of happiness. These have tended to show a U-shaped curve over time, with lowest levels of self-reported happiness among those aged in their mid 40s, while those in their 60s and 70s appear to be most happy. High heart rates and blood pressure seem to be correlated with unhappiness. Countries such as Denmark, Colombia and Mexico appear the happiest using self-reporting, while Korea and Japan are the unhappiest. Caution, however, should be applied to these findings as self-reports of happiness may be inaccurate, indicating cultural elements of stoicism, psychological denial, insouciance or bravado, rather than the honest reporting of happiness.

Many studies of happiness have failed to take into account the effects of mental illness and, especially, of *depression*. This is a common condition. In the general population of western countries there is a lifetime risk of clinical depression of 5 to 12 per cent in males, and 9 to 26 per cent in females. The two leading symptoms of clinical depression are *feeling sad* (or empty) and *diminished experiences of pleasure*. Others include losses of weight and appetite, insomnia, agitation, lethargy, feelings of worthlessness, recurrent thoughts of death and suicide, and impaired concentration. Are depressives to be included in the sampling of happiness levels? The lifetime risk in the US for abnormally *elevated* mood conditions is around 1 per cent. Both conditions are highly germane to happiness.

Governments clearly need to work to improve performance on the Big Seven happiness-promoters, although some (i.e. enjoying friends, family and personal values) are definitely not areas where governments should over-intrude. In these three cases governments need to 'set the scene' so that families, friendships and personal values can flourish without the government interfering in individual choices (provided these are within the law). Limits should be imposed upon behaviour (e.g. protecting family members from violence) but the details should be left to individuals. Governments also have a responsibility to encourage generally, but not to raise public desires and expectations unrealistically. Buddhism has traditionally taught techniques for overcoming unhappiness through reducing desires. If our expectations and desires are too high we are constantly disappointed. Caring for others and for projects beyond ourselves have also been found to make us happier. So has being religious and believing in God although, of course, there are exceptions to this rule when piety has had the effect of promoting guilt, hatred, fear or war.

Free Will and Moral Responsibility

There is no doubt that our moral values, character and behavior are based upon the functioning of our brains. Interference with such functioning through changes in medication, hormones, external stimuli, illness or damage can affect all these things. Furthermore, research by Benjamin Libet and others has indicated that the brain decides on our actions a split second *before* we make any conscious decision. From these findings I conclude that freedom of will is an illusion. However, the workings of the brain are partly subject to the strange laws of quantum mechanics that include notions of uncertainty, action-at-a-distance, field effects, probability, interference, super- position, multiple universes and the influence of conscious observation upon the physical world.

We end up not knowing what is meant by moral responsibility. Perhaps culpability has become an obsolete concept. If behaviour is necessitated by the laws of physics and biochemistry operating within our brains, then it appears that nobody is able to behave differently from the way that they do behave. This seems to make a nonsense of the idea of moral responsibility. Yet moral beliefs can clearly influence behaviour and we certainly feel as though we have the freedom to choose differing courses of action. But research has shown that our brain's decisions to act in fact occur a fraction of a second before we are conscious of making such decisions. Events at a submicroscopic scale are often unpredictable and can appear to have a freedom of their own. So are we mere spectators of our brain's quantum behaviour? Is the 'freedom' we feel in exercising our will, actually the same thing as quantum uncertainty itself, but experienced 'from the inside'? We cannot answer such questions at the present time. Painism is, however, no more compromised by such problems than is any other moral theory.

Some Current Moral Issues

Each age has its typical ethical issues. In Victorian times there was much debate about temperance, fidelity and honour. Between the world wars it was about social justice, imperialism and war itself. After the moral conservatism of the 1950s came the conceptual revolutions of the 1960s with timely attacks on sexism, racism, classism and, finally, on speciesism. Green matters in general came to the fore; nuclear issues too. Later it was questions over abortion, euthanasia and genetic engineering. There were also some perennial debates over matters such as sexual behaviour and the conduct of war which continued decade after decade enflamed by media interest and events themselves. I will briefly consider some of these topics below. In my books *Putting Morality Back into Politics* (2006) and *Painism : A Modern Morality* (2001) I have tried to look at how the application of painism might affect our evaluation of a range of such issues. Painism's emphasis upon reducing the suffering of individuals has led me to propose a number of tentative suggestions:

Media Ethics

The British media, especially the tabloid press, have gained a reputation for sensationalism and ruthless interference in the private lives of their victims. Undoubtedly there is value in freedom of speech and, in particular, the freedom of the media to investigate and speak out against political dishonesty and the abuses of power. The liberty of the press is, as Mill said it was, 'one of the securities against corrupt or tyrannical government'[11] yet this has sometimes been used as an excuse for great cruelty towards individuals. Because their audiences enjoy scandal, and particularly sexual scandal, journalists have frequently exposed the sexual lives of others as a means to sell their product. The media have justified such prurience on the doubtful grounds either of moral outrage or of weighty public interest. Neither justification has been clearly demonstrated. Two arguments have been more openly used to defend the media: the first is that the suffering of an individual when their sexual peccadilloes are exposed is of less moral importance than the alleged benefits to the large number of those who learn about it. What these benefits are has rarely been explained and the common allegation that sexual activity in politicians is linked with political incompetence or financial dishonesty has certainly never been supported by historical or sociological evidence. Above all, there is the hidden implication that the agony of the few matters less than the titillation of the masses. The second justification for media prurience has been the argument that a celebrity has, in some sense, signed away their right to privacy. Why is this the case? If a woman is interested in politics why should she lose her privacy? If a man is naturally skilled as a footballer why should his perfectly normal and consenting relationship with a woman be a matter for relentless and cruel media attention? Because Diana Spencer married royalty had she in any way 'consented' to the abandonment of her privacy? No. Yet self-interested and logically-challenged journalists regularly make such claims.

Over at least fifty years some of the British media appear to have become increasingly cynical and negative in their outlook. For example, when discussing the victories of the

---

[11] John Stuart Mill, *Essay on Liberty*, J. Gray (Ed), Open University Press, 1991

English cricket team over the Australians in 2010, journalists on the BBC's leading *Today* programme could only address themselves to the question 'what has gone wrong with the Australians?' rather than 'what has gone right with the English?' Being positive, giving praise, rejoicing at success are not within the normal range of responses for some of the British media. Constant interruptions from radio interviewers have made it difficult for respondents to finish the serious points they are trying to make. The role of the interviewer should be to elucidate, facilitate and to reveal the truth rather than constantly attacking, twisting and interrupting. Positive rather than negative. By being so often negative some of the media are poisoning the culture and causing widespread cynicism and unhappiness.

The quality of some British media reporting has certainly deteriorated over the years. It has 'dumbed down' and become increasingly sensationalised, personalised and trivialised. News has been converted into entertainment. It seems that financial reward is all that ultimately matters for sections of the media. Truth and the accuracy of reporting have been thrown overboard in the interests of predictable press cynicism and sensationalism. Take, for example, the disturbomg case of the brilliant economist and politician who, as First Secretary to the Treasury, was attempting to stabilise the British economy in 2010. The media revealed that he had claimed official expenses for the rental of rooms belonging to a male friend. This would be permitted under the rules unless that friend was either a spouse or a 'partner'. Under media pressure the man was forced to admit a nine year long 'relationship' with his landlord. They were not spouses, but were they 'partners' according to the rules? They did not entirely share their social lives. So does a sexual relationship define partnership? What sort of sex is necessary to incur this label? A kiss? Copulation? Fellatio? If so, how often or for how long does such a relationship have to exist to qualify as 'partnership'? In the case of a promiscuous person who sleeps with a dozen lovers are they *all* 'partners'? (They would be in medical terms.) Imagine the case of a politician who rents an apartment in a large block where the owner lives in a separate apartment. They may know each other and be friends. They live in this block together for many years. Are they 'partners'? If not, suppose they once had sex — are they then transformed into 'partners' for ever? Even if they subsequently quarrelled and did not ever have sex again? Or suppose they made up their quarrel and then had sex once more would they then become partners again? Or would they be deemed to have been partners all along? Or suppose one shared the other's flat for a few weeks without having sex — would they now be partners? What is the relevance of sex here anyway? Why does having sex with someone disqualify an MP from receiving expenses? Is it really any business of the state (or the media) to decide such matters?

Clearly the situation is irrational and ambiguous. Yet the sensationalist British press had no hesitation in condemning him out of hand, despite thereby possibly endangering the national interest and causing intense personal suffering. Nor did attractive young female reporters, wired with hidden microphones, have any compunction about tricking their way into a member of Parliament's constituency surgery by fraudulently passing themselves off as constituents, and questioning him about his attitudes towards their employer, an over-powerful foreign press tycoon. This was, in my view, immoral behaviour that should be made illegal. If a foreign government had done this it would have provoked an international incident. Because it was done by a section of the British press, nobody dared even to question it!

Looked at in moral terms, sections of the media have become as much of a menace as a benefit to the free society. The public often believes the media and in so doing people have been made cynical and superficial in their outlook generally. Much confusion about sexual morality has been actively cultivated by some of the media. There are already justifiable restraints on reporting through laws against racism, libel and the provocation of violence and criminality. It may be that these need to be augmented with penalties for gross inaccuracy, political bias and the causing of pain to individuals. In Britain, the electronic media (but not the written nor the new internet media) are already required by law not to show political bias. Advertisers and charity campaigners are required to tell the truth. Why cannot these restraints of truthfulness and impartiality be imposed upon *all* media and, especially, on the press?

Public Interest

One of the excuses given for the violation of privacy by the press is the so-called 'public interest'. When public funds, abuse of power or public safety are involved this may be a valid excuse, but too often it has been used to justify telephone-tapping and the prurient exposure of private sexual behaviour. The implication that the interests (or rights) of a *member of the public* per se count for more than the same interests (or rights) of a *politician* or *footballer* is surely unsound. There is nothing special about a 'member of the public' that gives them enhanced or reduced moral standing. Also unsound is the vague suggestion that the interests of the many ('the public') count for more than the interests of the few; here we are back with the Utilitarian (and democratic) mistake of adding up the titillations of the many and claiming that their *total* outweighs morally the great suffering of one or two individuals.

The use of the word 'public' suggests that millions of individuals are being affected. The danger lies in the implication that however slight the benefits are in each case, because there are millions of them they will add up to such a huge total that they are bound to justify the agony of one or a few individuals. It is sometimes claimed that the greater the majority the more this justifies the oppression of the individual. This is quite wrong.

Sexual Ethics

Thanks largely to the media's lucrative interest in the subject, sexual matters continue to be subjects for confused ethical debate. Homosexuality has become widely accepted except by the traditional religions, and modern contraception and medicines have rendered most forms of sexual intercourse relatively safe and acceptable.

Furthermore, greater knowledge of sexuality has reduced mistakes due to ignorance. As a source of so much intense human pleasure why, then, should sex be a subject for moral restraints of any sort? Is it merely a hangover of outdated prejudices and taboos that makes it so? Provided consent is given, should not sexuality be approved in every case? We are naturally erotic and promiscuous. Of course, there are still taboos against apparently consenting paedophilia, incest, bestiality and sadism but the arguments for such taboos can be shaky. Children are as interested in sex as adults are but are considered to be more vulnerable to being emotionally hurt. Is this true? Could they not give informed consent? Children who have been abducted and kept as emotional and sexual slaves sometimes do not feel entirely negatively about such experiences.[12] Of course, sex can cause emotional pain that is even greater than its pleasure. But how much of such pain is caused by society itself through religious teaching or an outdated disapproval of sex that generates guilt and shame? Or through our culture's encouragement of jealousy, envy and possessiveness? Or through the prosecution of offenders? So much fear of being found out is generated in paedophiles that they are sometimes driven to kill their victims or themselves. It is the violence and fear of violence, not sexual experiences themselves, that usually cause the trauma for abducted children. The fact that these issues can still create such hysteria suggests that they touch upon unresolved neurotic anxieties and frustrated urges in many people. The whole subject is still infused with irrationality and needs further de-mystification. We are still unsure whether sex is a glorious natural instinct to be enjoyed or something foul and uncivilised to be suppressed. It is clear that the sexual revolution of the 1960s is only half completed. At the end of the day morality should be about the pleasure, pain and happiness of others, and nothing else.

---

[12] Natascha Kampusch: *3,096 Days*, Penguin, London, 2010 and Margaux Fragoso, *Tiger, Tiger*, Penguin, 2011

How far is the deep pain caused by rejection, or the ending of a liaison, an artefact of our culture? The tendency to become emotionally attached to a person with whom a sexual relationship is established is less a feature of Western life than it used to be. Women, who seemed more vulnerable than men to such attachments in the past, now appear far more sexually confident, and thus less vulnerable. But attachment, which is part of the feeling of love, still needs to be understood and respected. As in all moral issues, pain is the subject upon which to focus.

In general, the reduced sense of sexual guilt in the West has increased happiness. This is particularly true of women who now seem far more fulfilled. Almost gone are the frustrated and neurotic spinsters of the past. Young women can now admit that they want sex and enjoy it without shame. When I began my career as a clinical psychologist I saw many people whose mental illness was partly or entirely caused by sexual guilt or sexual frustration. Years later, after the sexual revolution of the 1960s and 1970s, I have seen far fewer in this condition. The highly emotionally-suppressed culture of 1950s Britain was seething with unhappiness caused by the suppression of natural instincts such as sex. We do not want to go back there.

As far as pair-bonding is concerned a revolution is taking place. The old idea that living in pairs is naturally a desirable state is being challenged and many of the romantic and traditional ideas of love and marriage are now being viewed as mere fantasies. The experience of love—an intense and lasting obsession of one person for another—is increasingly being seen as equivalent to 'stalking' or as some other neurotic disorder. Love may merely be the product of an artificially inhibited society where the suppression of naturally promiscuous sexuality has fostered strange passions: delusions that can create great happiness but at the risk of bitter disillusionment and sorrow, and frequent annoyance for their 'victims'. Many societies have had no such romantic ideals in the first place, and have had no concept of marriage or of lasting one-on-one relationships. In some such societies men and women are not expected to fall in love at all. In others they are not expected to do so suddenly but may, after a carefully arranged marriage, grow into love gradually. Men want sex and women want children. Women want sex, too, but experience this need slightly differently from men. Because they are the parent most designed to care for offspring their sexual needs are more emotional and more long-lasting. They are programmed to need a mate, or someone, to stand by them for a year or two once they are pregnant, in order to provide protection and sustenance. In some cultures, and increasingly in our own, such support is provided not by the impregnator but by the state. In the past, protection came from the extended family. This craving for support is in the basic wiring of the female brain. The male brain is wired subtly differently with slightly less interest in offspring and with a greater emphasis upon new sexual partners. Sexual jealousy is strong in both genders, especially where attachment has been formed. The novelty, however, of an unfamiliar body is sexually exciting for women as well as for men but the need for permanence is stronger with women. Women instinctively flaunt their visible physical attractions, men instinctively respond by wanting to touch them and, if the male is acceptable, women instinctively respond to his touching.

Acceptability is influenced by a range of subtle social, emotional, aesthetic and hormonal conditions. Both sexes are often made happy by sex and by the feelings of affection and protectiveness for each other that arise partly as an automatic by-product of their sexual passion. While women crave protection and loyalty during their childbearing years, men equally naturally desire care and homely support as they mature. Whereas lust and promiscuity are probably associated with testosterone levels, long-lasting bonds are probably linked to levels of vasopressin and oxytocin.

I consider that there can be five basic but varying and interlocking psychological ingredients in a loving relationship:

- sexual attraction   (testosterone)
- affection   (dopamine)
- admiration/respect
- friendship
- attachment   (vasopressin and oxytocin)

I have added in brackets the brain chemicals that may be primarily associated with these sexual and loving experiences, in accordance with the findings of Lucy Brown and Helen Fisher. Love is certainly a complex mechanism with multiple components.[13] All are important sources of happiness for the individual and, when they fail, they can be heartrending causes of sorrow and despair. To these extents sex and love remain of interest to the ethicist. When considering sexual and loving behaviour the main moral issue, as always, is *suffering*.

Punishment and Crime

Why punish a crime? There are five usual answers to this question:

- deterrence of others
- deterrence of this particular criminal
- a sense of relief and security for the victim (and for society generally)
- some abstract idea of justice (e.g. retribution) and
- an alleged spiritual benefit for the criminal.

John Stuart Mill's opinion was that 'the only purpose for which power can rightfully be exercised over any member of a civilised community against his will is to prevent harm to others. His own good, either physical or moral, is not a sufficient warrant'. If this is correct (as it surely is) then it would seem to rule out the last two answers above as well as providing a strong argument for decriminalising the taking of recreational drugs, not wearing seat belts, helping some-

---

[13] R A Bressan and J A Crippa: The Role of Dopamine in Reward and Pleasure Behaviour, *Acta Psychiatrica Scandinavica*, 111, June, 2005

one to rationally commit suicide and all forms of consenting sexual behaviour. The possession of pornography of certain types, in particular, should clearly not be an offence unless this can be shown to harm others.

Jesus' own teaching was to forgive our enemies and indeed to 'turn our other cheek' to them. Yet little of modern criminal justice appears to be consistent with this Christian ethic. Instead, it pampers some people's natural instinct for revenge. What is more, there seems to be no convincing case for punishment. Deterrence rarely works and can be hugely expensive for society. Prisons are hardly the best places for reform, indeed precisely the opposite — they tend to breed crime. We should be able to expect deterrence in each case but in practice this does not happen.

Recent debate over the rights of prisoners to vote has revealed an amazing degree of moral blindness among British politicians. The punishment is prison, not the removal of all basic rights. The Court's sentence is not to deprive an offender of the right to vote any more than it is to deprive him of the right to observe his religion, to have food and shelter or to be protected from torture. No Court has the moral right to remove all rights. Some politicians seem to imagine that someone committed to prison, say for theft or fraud, should be treated as a total non-person! But prisons are part of society and part of democracy. They are not outside the boundaries of civilisation — or should not be.

In the case of terrorism there is clearly a need for military protection. But there is also a need to try to understand the motives of the terrorists. Sometimes these are no more than the desperation of the deprived or the ambitions of the narcissist. Sometimes their motives are largely personal.[14] Misapplied religion plays a part and finds fertile soil wherever there is poverty, oppression and educational deprivation. The basic causes of terrorism are the same as underlie any civil unrest: human misery due to bad governance, envy, inequality, lack of freedom, fulfilment, democracy and rights. Western governments have failed to realise this and

---

[14] Richard D Ryder: *Nelson, Hitler and Diana : Studies in Trauma and Celebrity,* Imprint Academic, 2009

have spent insufficient resources on attacking these underlying causes.

Sending offenders to prison obviously has the advantage of stopping those individuals from committing further offences while in prison. The protection of the public is thus achieved. Painism helps us here by focusing our attention upon *the sufferings of the victims of crime*, and on the reduction of these sufferings, rather than being led astray by abstract notions of retribution, justice or alleged spiritual benefits for criminals. It suggests that a *far greater emphasis upon the care of victims* would be appropriate and on the analysis and removal of the underlying motives for crime, terrorism and violence generally. Police forces often need to be reminded that their central mission should be *the protection of the public*, not the conviction of offenders, nor the protection of the state. In many advanced countries police lose sight of this, failing, for example, to protect ordinary individuals who are known to be in danger of attack.

Just War

The history of Christianity is the history of the gradual corruption of a decent and gentle morality into a violent and selfish one. Nowhere is this more clearly illustrated than in Christianity's attitude to war. In the first few centuries after Jesus, Christianity eschewed almost any form of violence but after its Romanisation by Constantine moral attitudes began to change. Constantine saw the Christian god chiefly as a powerful ally in battle and subsequent Christian teachers began to trim Christianity's moral code accordingly. Augustine even justified torture and the killing of innocents in war and in 1096 the Pope launched the First Crusade as a holy war that allowed the wholesale butchery of 'heathen' men, women and children.

A distinction was, however, made between a *holy war* where no quarter was given and a *just war* where some was. Thomas Aquinas proposed three moral conditions to attach to the latter. It is right to go to war, he said, provided there is:

- a just cause

- legitimate authority, and
- right intention

Later, the Catholic church in America added four other alleged essentials to this list insisting that:

- war must only be a last resort
- the suffering and death it causes must be proportionate to the death and suffering that caused the war
- there must be a reasonable probability of success
- the justice of both sides' claims must be compared.

All these seven (*jus ad bellum*) conditions have, however, proved very hard to define in practice. Two of the most crucial and difficult have been *just cause* and *proportionality*. Just cause has often been interpreted as self-defence or the defence of an oppressed victim.

As regards moral conditions for conduct once the war has started (*jus in bello*), the two most important have been taken to be :

- proportionality
- discrimination

Proportionality argues that the way warfare is conducted should not be out of proportion to the causes of the war. So a small territorial threat, for example, should not be settled with nuclear force. *Discrimination* refers to the requirement to discriminate between civilians and military personnel, and between the deliberate targeting of apparent innocents and those actually fighting.

Painism has difficulty with any principle that attaches weight according to the quantity of those affected, and is concerned instead about the *degree of suffering* of every affected individual. Because war almost inevitably causes severe suffering to innocent individuals painism is against almost any war. Principles such as proportionality in the conduct of war make little sense in painist terms, nor do arguments about right intention. Painism's concern is about the intensity of suffering of each individual and not about the numbers killed or wounded, or their motives. War may one day become morally permissible only if waged by the United Nations (as the only legitimate authority), using non-painful methods and ultra smart weapons that hit only combatants, as a last resort and justified only by the need to stop severe pain being inflicted.

Abortion

All procedures which cause pain for the foetus are wrong prima facie. After it attains painience, the foetus must be treated as a painient individual with all the moral (and practical) protection that this entails. When is a foetus painient? Clearly, the benefit of the doubt should always be given to the potential sufferer. If, at twenty-four weeks, say, a foetus is painient then it should have rights. The rights of a foetus are the same as those of an adult of the same level of painience who cannot give consent. In fact there is evidence that some cortical connections, believed to be necessary for the conscious experience of pain, are not established prior to twenty-four weeks.

Banking

The great scandals of 2008 onwards have raised some moral questions. The conduct of bankers has considerable consequences for others. Their risky and irresponsible behaviours have caused recession and unemployment. Their arrogant payments to themselves of large salaries and huge bonuses have provoked envy and outrage. In other words, the bankers have caused widespread and extreme unhappiness to others, especially through recession, loss of jobs and by creating comparisons with their own affluent lifestyles. Furthermore, many bankers seem morally illiterate. Their greed, obsession with money and addiction to the excitement of dealing in high stakes have created a feeling of insecurity among some of the rest of the population. How can all our fates be in the hands of such reckless people? They seem to have lost touch with reality and to be living in a dangerous world of fantasy. They were so stupid that many did not even understand the risks they themselves were taking.

Indeed, some were so dumb that they imagined they were supremely clever! They even thought they were irreplaceable. Such bankers have done far more damage to the economy of Great Britain and other countries than have Saddam Hussein, Al Quaeda and the Taliban all rolled up together! Are they arrested? No, they are given further bonuses! Some at least should have been detained and re-educated. Clearly, a new set of rules is needed creating a number of punishable offences for bankers who step out of line. Above all they should be trained in ethics and subjected to constant ethical oversight and, they should be educated to feel responsible for the effects that their actions have upon the happiness of others.

Euthanasia

As a general rule we should adopt the precautionary principle that, wherever painience is uncertain in a living animal it should be assumed to exist. Wherever a dying person who is neither under pressure from others nor clinically depressed has indicated clearly and repeatedly that they wish to die then they should be helped to do so. It is outrageous and cruel that the state thinks it has the right to prevent this. There is a duty upon those caring for the dying not only to administer enough analgesics to remove all pain but also to administer all appropriate psychoactive drugs so as to enhance the patient's sense of wellbeing until they die. Of course patients need to be protected from unscrupulous people who may benefit from their early demise. But they also may need assistance in reducing their suffering and easing their dying. Perhaps doctors have a duty not only to alleviate pain but to induce euphoria. Ending a life happily is more important than being happy earlier on. It is a disgrace that many governments have failed to arrange for the possibility of 'safe' euthanasia, continuing to harass those who compassionately try to assist, thereby increasing the sufferings of the dying. The business of the state is to help, not to hinder.

Divorce

In divorce the concern of the state should be primarily with the protection from suffering of children and the disabled. The state should provide no incentives, financial or other, to persuade individuals either to marry or divorce. Current divorce laws that require a spouse who does not seek divorce to pay a settlement to the spouse who does, are often immoral.

Bullying

Any behaviour, such as bullying, which causes severe unnecessary pain should, prima facie, be an offence in law. Bullying is a serious matter, both psychologically and morally. Research has shown that bullying, including bullying by siblings, is a powerful cause of pain and unhappiness.

The Welfare State

The provision of measures by the state to reduce the suffering of individuals is the twentieth century's greatest political achievement. The failure of states effectively to apply existing technology to treat the mentally and physically ill and to relieve their sufferings is currently one of the greatest immoralities. Painism very much approves of the welfare state.

Torture

The deliberate infliction of unconsented to and severe pain is the essence of evil. A line has to be drawn between the mild and usual pain caused by civilised detention in prison and the unacceptable pains caused by deliberate torture. The hypothetical case where there is the possibility that torture will cause reductions in the even greater sufferings of others, remains hypothetical and provides no substantial justification. In particular, painism denies that the agony of one individual can be justified by the *accumulated* minor benefits to many. The quantity of possible beneficiaries is morally irrelevant. Besides, torture can often produce misleading information that can, itself, produce further suffering. The torture produces present pain that is *certain*, while its alleged future benefits always remain *uncertain*. Painism recognises that pains and pleasures that are certain weigh far more than uncertain ones. Torture is quintessentially evil.

Political Theory

The business of government should be centred upon the reduction of the sufferings of others and the enhancement of their happiness. The infliction of pain through taxation, for example, is not justified unless the revenue is effectively spent on the reduction of the severe pains of the worst-off, i.e. the maximum sufferers of all ages, sexes, races and species. So spending tax money (including that which is raised painfully from low earners) to pay inflated salaries to public servants, or bonuses to bankers, for instance, is grossly immoral.

Democracy is morally deficient in that it promotes tyranny by the majority, based upon Utilitarianism. This should be rejected in favour of basing political right and wrong upon the reduction of the pains of the maximum sufferers (see pp 134–139). Individuals matter. Corporations and institutions such as banks need to be morally restrained. There is also a need for ethical foreign policies. When a tyrant is unjustly causing severe suffering to individuals (even his own citizens) then we, the world community, have a duty to interfere and to bring such a tyrant to book. But we can hardly be justified in doing this if, in the process (such as the invasion of Iraq in 2003), we cause pain to others which is even greater than that being caused by the tyrant.

It has become fashionable to talk about the 'size' of government, by which is meant the extent to which the state interferes in the lives of citizens. In a dictatorship the state may control what a citizen can do and say. In an anarchy the individual may have complete freedom but runs the risk of starvation, lack of welfare services and civil disorder and violence. In both these extremes there is fear: fear of the power of the state on one hand and fear of unruly individuals on the other. Neither condition is conducive to happiness. Some compromise seems desirable, and democracy has much to commend it. But, in a modern democracy there is still room for differences in approach to the question of state 'size'. How far should citizens be in control of education, police and health services? Should central government remain in control of detailed operations at local level? Can local government, often insufficiently democratic or talented, be put in charge? Or should 'the third sector' of charities and other unofficial volunteer bodies be empowered to participate? Should the individual citizen be encouraged in new ways to join in the decision-making processes?

Painism may be able to make some suggestions here. The immediate objective for painism is the reduction of the sufferings of maximum sufferers, then of all those affected, ultimately to zero. This is in the context of the overall drive for the happiness of individuals. By emphasising the negative (i.e. the suffering), painism indicates that there is a real distinction between the provision of positive pleasures and the reduction of pains. It is the latter function surely (the reduction of pains), that should be the function of *the state* through the provision of welfare benefits and health services. Defence services, too, as a protection against the sufferings caused by external attack, are another legitimate role for the state. All these functions are suffering-reduction or suffering-avoidance functions. Where the private sector can play a far more active role is in the provision of positive pleasures such as in the arts, music and entertainment. Many individuals derive pleasure from being involved in decision-making and such citizens should be encouraged to join in the running of the state through more frequent referenda and in other more hands-on ways. This in itself will promote their happiness. The police need to be re-educated so that they see themselves not as agents of state authority but as servants of the citizen, not as prefects but protectors. So in their case also there are strong reasons for greater citizen control and involvement. Other than overseeing their probity the state, and its relevant agencies, should lift off their controls over charities. The role of the state here should be to help the charities in whatever ways they can, and not in undermining their work with petty and expensive regulations and prohibitions.

Sexism and Ageism

The moral message is this: reject all forms of prejudice and discrimination that are based upon moral irrelevancies such as age and gender. As far as painism is concerned the sufferings of males and females are of equal importance morally, as are those of the old and young.

Religion

Religion has become a controversial topic in recent years. Attacks from atheists and agnostics have become more publicised and the scandals of child-abuse by priests on one hand and religiously-garbed terrorism on the other have caused some established religions to lose credibility. Ironically, this is because offending members of these religions *have upset not just their religious colleagues, but the moral sensibilities of the global secular community*, demonstrating that there is a growing international consensus, that is independent of any religion, about what is morally right. What is this consensus? I would suggest it is *a respect for the happiness of others and a concern for their pain*. The theory of painism is merely the technical and detailed expression of this.

I hope the growing tsunami of atheism in Europe will not sweep away what is good about the old religions. Certainly we can do away with their cruelties and prejudices. There is no room for the vicious sectarian conflicts of the past, nor their murderous crusades, nor the bloody persecution of heretics; nor for absurd, outdated and often hurtful religious bigotries as regards gender, species, sexual orientation, sexual behaviour and contraception.

Religion's three psychological functions — providing magic (power), meaning (purpose) and morality, vary in strength over the centuries. First one function is in the ascendancy and then another. Wherever religion becomes extreme in its power- mode it goes wrong. Yet there is another side to be found in most of the great religions of the world — a peacefulness, a warmth and a gentleness. This is its moral mode. Many call this aspect its 'spirituality', others simply its 'compassion' or its 'love'. Such love is the good side of all the great religions. It needs to be emphasised and retained.

Whether it is right to teach religion to children is, however, debatable. Is it right at all to teach bogus 'truths'? Would it be right solemnly to teach beliefs in fairies, dragons or vampires? We can never be sure that such beliefs will enhance the lives of believers nor of others around them. In the happiness stakes, the record of religion is a mixed one, although having a morality itself may, on the whole, be conducive to happiness. Morality can, however, be independent of religion and can be taught without the untestable and irrational metaphysics of faith that accompanies the religious approach, and this is one of the messages of this book. The visit of Pope Benedict to Britain in 2010 raised the issue of the alleged growing immorality and ungodliness of Europe. In particular, the pope attacked the increasingly 'aggressive secularism' of Britain and its 'marginalisation' of religion. Young people should grow up wanting to be like saints rather than celebrities, he suggested, reminding them that 'true happiness is to be found in God'. What he assumed, it seems, is that religion is the only basis for morality and the only source of true happiness. Both assumptions are clearly wrong. Religion can indeed induce happiness in some, but for many others it can become a source of guilt, hatred, frustration and misery. Certainly, religion can be a basis for morality but there are also secular bases, such as painism's, that are more convincing for people today. It has been suggested that religion can sometimes make people happy. (It can also do the opposite and I have seen patients driven to despair by religion.) It is suggested that where religion helps people to be happy is where it provides 'a meaning for life'. What does 'a meaning of life' actually mean? It seems to indicate that existence has a value or purpose outside that of the individual. People felt happy under Hitler for this reason. Conforming, going along with an ideal, pleasing a real or imagined figure of authority. This is the Meaning or Purpose component in religion; it obviates the need for further thought (which can be stressful).

Equality

Equality is not a political or moral ideal that is as often discussed as it used to be. As a source of suffering it is, however, relevant. Painism would support equalities of opportunity in society, and the idea that there should be 'safety nets' to ensure that the least advantaged should be lifted by the state (or by charity) above those minimum levels where suffering becomes significant. Taking more money from the very rich (through taxation) may be justifiable if such revenues are spent upon health, education and other services, but not merely for the principle of equality itself. Equality's only merit is as a reducer of pain.

Fairness

The recession of 2008 revealed the discrepancies in income in British society: on one hand near subsistence living and, on the other, the huge salaries paid to directors and public officials, some paid from the public purse, and the vast bonuses that numerous greedy and corrupt bankers paid to themselves. These revelations prompted a new public discussion of fairness, and a debate ensued about the 'unfair' privileges of gender, age, wealth, occupation, education and class. There were calls for more progressive taxation that would hit the rich far harder than the less well off. Threatened with the cuts to social services announced in 2010, attacks were again made on sexism, ageism and classism. The allegedly unfair advantages of being a celebrity were also widely attacked. By *fairness* most people meant there should be *fair and equal opportunities*, and no advantages attached to class, ethnicity, age, gender, wealth, occupation or any other attribute, except *hard work*. Effort, industriousness and diligence emerged as the only acceptable grounds for privilege. Should innate skills and abilities also be highly rewarded? This remained an area of uncertainty, and there seemed little attempt to correlate financial reward with productivity or the provision of services to society. Painism might suggest that those who most directly and effectively reduce the sufferings of others (e.g. carers, nurses and doctors) deserve to be better rewarded than bureaucrats or bankers. Speciesism, too, is unfair.

Civil Violence

Political protest sometimes leads to damage to property, certain other breaches of the law and injury to protesters, bystanders and police. Are they justified? Debates on this topic are often confused. First it is necessary to distinguish beween:

- non-violent political protest
- violent political protest

Most of us can agree that non-violent protest is nearly always permissible unless it causes harm to others. Then a distinction has to be made between violence to:

- material property (windows, cars, statues etc.)
- 'guilty' persons
- innocent bystanders
- police (e.g. police horses, police dogs, *et al.*)
- others

The wrongness of violence is to be judged by the pain it causes. Violence against non-painient objects causes no pain per se but it *can* cause suffering indirectly e.g. sadness to the owner of a car or a window destroyed by rioters. To this extent violence to property is wrong but it is less wrong than violence towards painient individuals such as protesters, bystanders, police or police horses. Violence towards persons is a serious moral matter.

Is it justified if the object of violence is considered in some way to be *guilty* e.g. a politician who is held responsible for an unpopular policy or a banker considered to have partly been the cause of a recession?

The answer must be 'no' because, in an efficient democracy, it is not legitimate for a rioter either to decide guilt or to impose punishment. These matters are properly decided by the Courts. The injury of police or their horses by protesters similarly cannot be condoned unless the police act in a way that is either:

- grossly provocative, or
- a threat to the safety of protesters or others

If the protesters are not peaceful does this justify violence by the police?

In a modern state the police should be sufficiently well protected and trained not to respond to violence with violence. By virtue of their position the police are *more*, and not less, culpable for their violence than is the ordinary citizen. The police are supposed to be the protectors of society. They should intervene to protect life and limb, not to threaten them. Police should never attack nonviolent protesters. Protesters are also a part of society. Harmless and unpainful devices such as tear-gas and water cannon may be justifiable under certain conditions but these conditions need to be published in advance and protesters allowed to avoid such methods being used against them. Violence in self-defence or the defence of others should always be the minimum required.

Is it justifiable for protesters to break the law if the law has been passed democratically? As a general principle morality trumps legality, and especially where laws are made that ignore the rights and interests of minorities. However, where the law is broken the consequent punishment has to be expected. It is reasonable to believe that respect for the law reduces the probability of a more generalised state of anarchy developing that would cause widespread and severe suffering.

In general, the violence of a riot is far more *certain* to cause pain than it is to reduce it. Therefore, the attempted suppression of cruelty or oppression by means of violent protest is not usually justified unless it is a last resort, all others having failed. The pain caused by a violent protest (such as a thrown brick, a bomb or a bullet) is almost certain to occur, while the pain reduced by such protest remains highly uncertain and in the future. Painism attaches far more importance to the certain effects of today than to the uncertain pipe-dreams of the future.

Police

There has been too little discussion of the philosophy of policing. Basically, the police exist in order to protect the public. They do not exist to protect some sections of society against others nor to protect the state, the government nor any particular customs, attitudes or values. The police act within the law at all times. They should be impartial, independent of the media, transparent, fair, kind and respectful towards all individuals, regardless of class, ethnicity, age, gender, religion or species. In Britain, the police act under the sovereignty of Parliament and not at the operational direction of the government itself. The police role is to maintain security and to enforce the law. They should respect the pluralism, diversity and popular deliberation of a democratic society. They do not act politically and they respect the civil rights and liberties of all persons including the suspected and convicted. In a democracy their conduct should be transparent and under independent civilian oversight. Their salaries are paid by the taxpayer and they are the servants of the people and not their masters. They exist to help and not to harm. In an era of terrorism and passionate minority dissent this raises inevitable tensions between human rights (e.g. against intrusion, infiltration, telephone tapping, unfair detention and search etc.) on one hand and effective intelligence and security on the other. These difficulties need to be openly and frequently debated. It is not pleasant to live in a society where green campaigners are spied upon by police, their groups infiltrated and their telephones tapped. This is the beginnings of a police state. On the other hand, painism sees the police as potentially key figures in the relief of pain and distress.

Environmentalism

The state of the environment hugely influences the happiness of all painient beings. Painism does not demand that all *natural* things per se (e.g. rocks, rivers and mountains), nor all *living things* (e.g. including trees and other plants not considered to be painient) nor all *human-made* features of the environment (such as buildings), should be regarded as ends in themselves. If they themselves cannot suffer, they are of value only in as much as they cause pain or pleasure to painient beings. All painient things deserve respect, of course, not just the human species.

Faith Schools

Should religion, which is not based upon fact and can contain potentially divisive messages, be taught in schools? There is a strong case against. Clearly there is a need for children to be taught about right and wrong, but does this have to be in a religious rather than a secular context? No. Does this moral teaching have to be dogmatic rather than in the form of rational discussion? No. Of course, religion can itself be a source of happiness for some—the opium of the people—but this should never be at the expense of others. In Britain the main political parties have approved the founding of faith-based schools even though, in some cases, such schools are permitted to exclude children they consider not to be of the correct faith. Such education, founded as it is upon religious discrimination, is a recipe for social division in the long term. The example of Northern Ireland should have been enough warning. Just as the idealistic promotion of minority languages in schools, so also the teaching of religion in schools should be things of the past. The history of Europe for thousands of years has been the history of religious conflict and atrocity. Parents understandably want their children to have a grounding in morality but why does this have to be wrapped up in the irrationalities of religion? Far better, surely, that children be exposed to the secular philosophies of Greece and Rome, of secular Buddhism and of secular ethical philosophy since the Enlightenment, including humanism and painism.

Foreign Affairs

Should a nation interfere on moral grounds in the affairs of another state? For several centuries this has been considered to be a bad thing to do. Yet surely there are compelling cases. Take the Serbian murdering of Moslems in the 1990s, or the stoning to death of adulteresses in Iran in the present century, or the continued killing of whales by the Japanese, or the persecution of Jews by the Nazis. Of course, where there is a strong moral argument for interference, normal diplomatic measures, independently or through the United Nations, are available. But some may say it is up to the Iranian authorities to punish their own offenders as they see fit, and that what went on within the boundaries of the Third Reich was solely a matter for Hitler to decide. We seem to be getting close here to the relativistic argument (see p ...) that other societies have different ideas as to what is right and wrong, and should be allowed to act upon them. If we do not accept this relativism and assert, for instance, that the rights of humans or animals, *wherever* they are, are still our concern, then we do appear to have a right to intervene. This might apply not only to offences committed by dictators against their citizens but also to offences committed by foreign citizens themselves. So if, like the USA, we have the power and resources to act as the world's policeman, should we behave in this way—arresting bank robbers in Rowanda, paedophiles in Patagonia and cat torturers in Katmandu? If we honestly believe that these offences are morally wrong, and if we have the approval of the United Nations, then why should the formalities of artificial national frontiers make much difference? After all, victims usually do not *choose* to be citizens of one state or another. It is not their fault that they are being persecuted in a way altogether different from the way in which they would be treated in other countries. Fortunately, international law also seems to be slowly moving in this direction—towards the idea of one global code enforceable by the international courts or the United Nations or, where that fails, by individual state action. Morals, surely, should have spatial consistency. They apply to suffering creatures wherever they are—whether in Iran, upon Mars or at the bottom of the sea. The fact that moral customs differ from culture to culture is no proof that some moral judgements are not correct. So a universalist and ethical foreign policy seems to me to be a reasonable thing to aim for when it comes to suffering. Yes, we do have a duty to non-violently persuade other peoples and other governments to act morally.

Was the West correct to intervene in Iraq in 2003? That was a use of force. It was a violent intervention that led to the deposing of a tyrant but at the cost of tens of thousands of lives, many of them innocent. Surely there can be no justification for killing or maiming innocent civilians in order to rid them of their dictator. It would have been better if he had been arrested in an orderly manner by the equivalent of a United Nations police force, without undue cost to others. The private sector, too, needs to be controlled in the West's relationship with unsavoury regimes. The use of western public relations companies by dictators, for example, should be registered by governments and be dependent upon the truth. Where a private PR company tells lies on behalf of their clients they should be deregistered and punished. Where private security agencies are employed they should be subject not only to the laws of the state that employs them, but also subject to ethical regulations at home.

Maybe the constitution and performance of the United Nations itself need to be reformed, but the UN should also become more proactive in providing oversight and advice on good governance to Third World states.

As with the arguments in favour of a 'just war', however, we need to satisfy various conditions including:

1) proper authority (the United Nations)
2) minimal force
3) last resort
4) proportionality

Instead of just throwing money at unwholesome dictators, strings should be attached which increase the promotion of human rights, democracy and all goals consistent with painism.

Speciesism

We have said that speciesism is like racism or sexism — a prejudice based upon morally irrelevant physical differences. Speciesism is a form of bigotry. It is unintelligent and out of date. Since Darwin we have known that we are human animals related to all the other animals through evolution; how, then, can we justify our almost total oppression of all the other species? All animal species can suffer pain and distress. Nonhuman animals scream and writhe like us; their nervous systems are similar and contain the same biochemicals that we know are associated with the experience of pain in ourselves. So our concern for the pain and distress of others should be extended to any 'painient' (i.e. pain-feeling) individual regardless of his or her sex, class, race, religion, nationality or species. Indeed, if aliens from outer space turn out to be painient, or if we ever manufacture machines who are painient, then we must widen the moral circle to include them. Painience is the only convincing basis for attributing rights or, indeed, interests to others. Painience entails personhood. All painient creatures should thus be treated as 'persons', and persons deserve respect.

Several other qualities, such as 'inherent value' have been suggested as the qualification for moral status. But value cannot exist in the absence of consciousness or potential consciousness. Thus, rocks and rivers and houses, being unconscious, have no interests and no rights of their own. This does not mean, of course, that they are not of value to us, and to many other painients, including those who need them as habitats and who would suffer without them. Speciesism is often justified on the grounds that animals allegedly lack intelligence, autonomy or language. I have argued that this overlooks the crucial importance of painience. Greater size, intelligence, autonomy, alleged soulfulness, use of language or resemblance to the species Homo Sapiens are all morally irrelevant features that do not justify a higher moral status. We do not give greater moral status to taller people, professors, priests or linguists so why do we so often hear these arguments in support of speciesism? Not only animals but human babies and some who are severely disabled can also lack full intelligence, autonomy and language. Is their moral standing, therefore, to be reduced?

Of course, individuals from different species have different needs and reactions. What is painful for some is not necessarily so for others. So we can treat different species differently, but we should always treat equal suffering equally. In the case of nonhumans, we see them mercilessly exploited in factory farms, in laboratories and in the wild. A whale may take twenty minutes to die after being harpooned. A lynx may suffer for a week with her broken leg held in a steel-toothed trap. A battery hen lives all her life unable even to stretch her wings. An animal in a toxicity test, poisoned with a household product, may linger in agony for hours or days before dying. These are major abuses causing great suffering. Yet they are still justified on the grounds that these painients are not of the same species as ourselves. It is almost as if some people had not heard of Darwin! We treat the other animals not as relatives but as unfeeling things. We would not dream of treating our babies, or mentally handicapped adults, in these ways — yet

these humans are sometimes less intelligent and less able to communicate with us than are some exploited nonhumans. The simple truth is that we exploit the other animals and cause them suffering because we are more powerful than they are. Does this mean that if those aforementioned aliens landed on Earth and turned out to be far more powerful than us we would let them — without argument — chase and kill us for sport, experiment on us or breed us in factory farms, and turn us into tasty humanburgers? Would we accept their explanation that it was perfectly moral for them to do all these things as we were not of their species? Basically, it boils down to cold logic. If we are going to care about the suffering of other humans then logically we should care about the suffering of nonhumans too. It is the heartless exploiter of animals, not the animal protectionist, who is being irrational, showing an arrogant and unjustifiable urge to put his own species upon a pedestal. We all, thank goodness, feel a natural spark of sympathy for the sufferings of others. We need to catch that spark and fan it into a fire of rational and universal compassion. I am not saying that following the line taken by natural compassion automatically makes my actions good; only that where natural impulses direct us in the way of goodness we should use them as helpful drivers. Painism frequently surfs the waves of natural compassion in this way.

All of this has implications, of course. If we gradually bring nonhumans into the same moral and legal circle as ourselves then we will not be able to exploit them as our slaves. Much progress has been made with sensible new European legislation in recent decades, but there is still a very long way to go. Some international recognition of the moral status of animals is long overdue. There are various conservation treaties, but nothing at UN level, for example, that recognises the rights, interests or welfare of the animals themselves. That must, and I believe will, change.

An Overview

How far have we solved some of the problems raised in the first chapter? Many moral principles and ideals have been proposed over the centuries—justice, freedom, equality and brotherhood, for example. But I have claimed that these are mere stepping stones to the ultimate good which is happiness; and happiness is made easier by freedom from all forms of pain and suffering (we can use the words 'pain' and suffering' interchangeably). Indeed, if you think about it carefully you can see that the reason why these other ideals are considered important is that people have believed that they are essential to the banishment of suffering. In fact they do sometimes have this effect, although not always.

The future development of applied ethics will depend to a large extent upon the development of techniques to measure and compare the intensities of pains. But why emphasise pain and other forms of suffering rather than pleasure and happiness? One answer is that pain is much more powerful than pleasure. Would you not rather avoid an hour's torture than gain an hour's bliss? Another reason is that pain is more easily measured than is happiness. A third is that when any individual's overall state of consciousness becomes less and less painful it eventually reaches a point of neutrality where it is neither painful nor pleasurable. At this point onwards it seems less morally imperative for others to interfere. Of course it is good to give pleasure to an already contented individual but it seems more morally important to reduce the pain of a miserable person. I am suggesting, for example, that five units of pain reduction for an unhappy person matters more than five units of increased pleasure for an individual who is already fairly happy. Pain is the one and only true evil.

In the eighteenth century it was acceptable to talk of happiness. The United States was founded upon 'the pursuit of happiness' and in England Jeremy Bentham based Utilitarianism upon happiness. But, during the following century of imperialism and industry, talk of happiness seemed to smack of weakness. The Napoleonic wars and the building of Empire encouraged the British to cultivate militaristic asceticism, and discipline and self-control became the orders of the day among the ruling classes, while a puritanical religion encouraged hard work and salvation through the denial of the flesh. Two world wars accentuated these Spartan values and, as a topic for discussion, happiness became almost taboo until the end of the twentieth century.

Since the last few years of the twentieth century it has gradually become permissible again to talk of happiness as the chief object of government. Think-tanks such as the New Economics Foundation (NEF) now address such questions and have, following Aristotle, begun to concentrate upon what they have called the *hedonic* (reported as 'emotional') and *eudaimonic* (relating to the feeling of contentment derived from having a sense of purpose in life) aspects of happiness. Recently, the director of NEF, Andrew Simms, has attacked our 'long hours, throwaway, materialistic, individualistic, status-obsessed culture' and the NEF has published its five point plan for happiness, recommending that we:

- connect with family, friends and neighbours and invest time in developing these relationships
- be active (e.g. walking, running, gardening, dancing)
- take notice of our environment
- keep learning new things
- give to others, both emotionally and materially

Democracy and the Future of Governance

The central point in painism is the realisation that it is meaningless to total pains, pleasures and happinesses across individuals (see pp 75–80). This realisation has the effect, however, of invalidating the basis of democracy. (See 'the tyranny of the majority', pp 142–144)

Since the days of Plato democracy has been feared as mob-rule. Neither the British civil war nor the subsequent American and French revolutions wholeheartedly stood for democracy. The fear of the uneducated masses ran too deep. There was the widespread belief that democracy leads to populism, poor government and, at its worst, anarchy. In Britain 'democracy', like 'rights', remained a dirty word. As a series of reform laws widened the franchise during the nineteenth century, this fear of the ignorant masses led to a movement to raise state levels of education. Gradually the idea that the uneducated people should be democratically *represented* by an educated elite began to be superceded by Socialism, and by notions of a more *direct* democracy, and even of government by the people themselves. The subsequent belief that a career in politics is open to anyone and the feeling that elected politicians do indeed represent my interests and listen to my views are, surely, all valued sources of happiness in themselves. Socialism and Marxism were narrow-mindedly obsessed with equality and class struggle as if these were valid ends in themselves. These angry ideologies could not see that these aims were mere stepping stones to universal happiness. In America, human rights and democracy have now become the vision. But there are still some huge problems with democracy.

Reforms of Government : the Compassionate State

No country yet has a proper democracy. Democracy has many faults, and the most fundamental fault, as I have often said, is that democracy encourages tyranny by the majority. In other words democracy can impose suffering upon minorities and individuals in the interests of pleasing the majority. In democracy, the majority is always right. The only way the happiness of minorities can be safeguarded is by the rather haphazard application of a system of rights.

Some form of more direct democracy, where minority and individual rights can be better represented, is probably the most just form of government and the one most likely to promote happiness. In general, happiness is encouraged if people feel they have an influence in government; if they feel their views are being listened to. An election, especially if it is a non-proportional type, once every four years or so, is not sufficient. With modern electronic technology it should be possible for all citizens (even those who find technology difficult) to vote in frequent referenda. One problem for a push button democracy of this sort is that people are lazy or will not remember to press their buttons. This might be true especially when governance is good and the average citizen is not feeling unhappy. (Only when things go seriously wrong do many people become politically involved.) The other problem is how to fully inform citizen voters (without boring them) of all the arguments on all sides of each issue. This would be a formidable challenge. Plato warned against rule by the ignorant. But there could be ways around this problem, again through succinct and impartial electronic briefings from an independent agency.

Private money, too, should be entirely banished from the democratic process. Candidates and political parties (if these continue) should be funded fairly on a strictly regulated basis by the state alone. There is absolutely no excuse for parties to have their policies or decisions influenced by the whims of rich tycoons or single issue donors. The present British system (in 2010) is deeply corrupt and in the USA it is worse. Overall, of course, the central purpose of governments should be to increase the happiness of all individuals (of whatever race, gender or species) within their range of influence, not disproportionately those who fund them. Corruption may prove the greatest challenge to peace and happiness in the future. Cultures where corruption is established as a way of life are permeating the less corrupt cultures of the West. Highly corrupt states, or parts of states, are already affecting world sport and, as their economies grow, they threaten to corrupt the rest of the world, economically and in other ways. A worldwide campaign against corruption is clearly needed. It is hard to be happy in a corrupt society.

The moral future of the West to an extent seems to hinge upon an ethical struggle between an agnostic and progressive Western Europe and a fundamentalist religious America. Whereas between 70% and 80% of people in Europe (and the Far East) believe that humans have evolved along with the other animals, only 33% believe this in the USA. What explains this extraordinary anti-Darwinism in America? Almost certainly it is the rigid naivity of American religious belief. Why, then, is there this religiosity in the United States? Why is there this gullibility that leads apparently normal Americans to sincerely believe they have been abducted by aliens or chosen by God? Are Americans addicted to religion? It has been said unfairly that religion is now chiefly for the educationally deprived and intellectually challenged. But even some outstandingly educated and intelligent Americans openly proclaim their religious and moral conservatism, in a way that would provoke ridicule in Europe.

How can apparently rational adult human beings believe in all this stuff? Is religion a form of delusional disorder? Perhaps the answer lies in the historical origins of modern America. Founded largely by religious extremists it has been populated over the course of several centuries by immigrants who typically have included thousands of social misfits. Perhaps the only way the whole enterprise was kept together was by the old elite forcing religion upon the incomers! On the right wing of American politics today there appears to be difficulty in believing that those who lack religion (in the conventional sense) can be moral. For this reason perhaps, atheism is now feared as much as communism was in the last century. Some on the political right simply cannot grasp that atheists can be moral, altruistic and trustworthy. So we have today's paradox of the world's leading nuclear super-power posing as the champion of democracy and modernity, while being steered by Bronze Age moral belief systems!

Yet it does seem plausible that the West still has a role to play in world moral leadership. Despite the disgraceful behaviour of the Bush/Blair era, which has so severely damaged respect for the West, we have been experimenting with and thinking about morality and governance for several thousand years, and so may have some worthwhile answers. Europe may not exceed the up and coming economies of the world in terms of cash or commodities (including hard work) but only in terms of creativity and probity. Similarly, in moral and governance terms, we should be offering not old dogmas but open-mindedness and creative new ways forward.

Democracy is seen as an ideal by millions and as such has given a sense of purpose and pleasure to many. Furthermore, democracy has been shown to increase the happiness of individuals by allowing them to feel part of the decision-making process. Their self-worth is thereby enhanced. This is its main moral advantage. In practical or governmental terms, however, democracy has obvious disadvantages. It has been found that the masses are reluctant to vote for making sacrifices for the greater good or to vote for long-term rather than short-term policies. So, in general, the masses tend to vote for their own material short-term interests. Michael Portillo may opine that 'the untutored masses usually get it right'[15] but the evidence for this seems shaky. The democratic masses may feel happier than the subjects of a tyranny but they can also get practical decisions wrong. Modern government is a complex and highly technical business; how can non-experts be expected to get it right?

---

[15] Michael Portillo: BBC Radio 4, *Opinion*, 25 May 2010

Over one hundred countries in the world are now designated officially as being democratic and others are slowly moving in that direction. Authoritarian states are unstable but so also are new democracies. Instant democracies usually fail. They need time and proper assistance to build checks, balances and the attitudes of compromise, fairness and toleration that are required for a democracy to flourish. In China and India it is chiefly the rural poor who desire democracy while the middle classes, fearing the mob, prefer prosperity.

The main faults in Western democracies appear to be as follows:

- Unproportional electoral systems
- External funding leading to influence on policies
- Powers of patronage by parties that corrupt individual conscience
- Unelected bureaucracies
- Tyranny by majority

In both the United States and Britain, two of the self-proclaimed pioneers of modern democracy, the systems are far from flawless. Money totally distorts democracy in the United States, allowing rich men and corporations effectively to buy the policies they want. To a lesser extent this is also true of Britain. Until no politician or party is permitted to accept external sources of funding of any sort will we be rid of this systemic corruption. There is also the need for a properly representational electoral system, where votes are accurately reflected in seats. The powers of patronage by parties are also far too strong, stifling genuine debate in the legislatures. In Britain democracy has become eroded by bureaucracy and we have seen government by unelected and unanswerable QUANGOS. This is also very true of the European Union where the undemocratic nature of some of its institutions is glaringly obvious. Human rights legislation in Britain has also given increasing powers to the judiciary — themselves unelected. These are some of the problems that faced the Cameron-Clegg Coalition of 2010, challenging it to cleanse democracy and re-establish trust in politics in general. The answer may be a new 'compassionate state', but this will require, I believe, a different moral foundation for politics, such as that proposed by painism.

Democracy is better than anarchy, autocracy, plutocracy or a host of other types of government, but it still has faults. Where does the legislative authority ultimately reside in a modern democracy? Is it with the people? Should it be? The sovereignty of the Westminster Parliament, for example, is currently under threat from several quarters, including the EU, the assemblies of Scotland and Wales, and the new unelected Supreme Court. The actual power of the nation state is vitiated by growing globalisation, the United Nations, multinational corporations and the great international QUANGOs like the World Bank, the International Monetary Fund, NATO and the World Trade Organisation. Corruption, poor governance and increasing food prices are leading to revolutionary disturbances throughout the Islamic world. Such states need to become democracies. Democracy can still be seen as a first step towards a better society. Democracy's good points include transparency, elections and a greater respect for rights.

Democracy is also a good thing in so far as it tries to take everybody's wishes, and hence their welfare and happiness, into account. Of course, the preferences of nonhumans should also be included, but rarely are. Seeing an old newsreel of German tanks advancing into France in 1940 through a herd of cows I was struck to see not only the bold defiance of the French cows but, so I thought, the tanks' careful avoidance of them. If true, that was certainly as it should have been! There are hundreds of species of animal who are painient, not just our own.

The Duty to Protect

How far should we go to protect others from harm? Duties are the corollary of rights; they are the reverse side of the same coin. If you have the right to be protected from X, then

I have a duty to protect you from X. We have to be reasonable about this, however. Although I may have a duty to help, hands on, every peasant in China and every Koala in Australia, in practice I cannot be expected to spend my whole life travelling the globe trying to help everybody. Perhaps only those we encounter in the course of our ordinary lives should concern us.

However, when it comes to powerful states who have the resources to deal with thousands of cases across the world, the picture changes. If a state has the power to feed starving peasants five thousand miles away should it not do so? Broadly speaking, 'yes'. But should it interfere even if the relevant foreign government does not want it to do so? The traditional answer has always been 'No'! Today, such an attitude is beginning to look dated. The effects of television and the internet have made the world a smaller place. We feel close to people on the other side of the planet. If we know they are being badly treated we want to help them, and to hell with their governments' talk of not interfering in their internal affairs. These days, we particularly want to interfere when it is the foreign government itself that is causing its own citizens (human or nonhuman) grievous suffering. National boundaries are, after all, artificial contrivances. Nobody chooses to be born within a particularly political boundary. It is a matter of chance. It is not our fault if we are born under a dictatorship from which we cannot easily escape.

What, then, about the use of force? With the approval of the United Nations NATO intervened to protect the citizens of Kosovo and Libya, and various coalitions have intervened in order to protect the citizens of Kuwait and Kabul. Old-fashioned cynics, among them Mr Putin in Russia, have always looked for hidden motives for such interventions and yet, in the minds of thousands, the principal motive for these interventions has been simple altruism — a genuine compassion for the sufferings of others. Mr Putin should try to recognise this.

The UN agreement in 2011 to attack Libya from the air was to establish a 'no-fly' zone and to protect Libyan civilians. Not to act would have meant the imminent slaughter of civilians in Benghazi by President Gaddafi's forces.

The main ethical problem in such situations (as it was in Iraq) is that the act of protection itself can cause great suffering to innocent individuals. Indeed, any sort of force directed at persons is likely to cause them pain of some sort and this is disapproved of by painism. It is irrelevant, in a painist's view, whether a million are affected or only one. Thus very little force seems to be permitted under the rules of painism.

So how can we justify riding, in a knightly manner, to the rescue of distressed maidens, starving peasants or those oppressed by dictators? How can we justify intervening militarily to prevent hundreds of Muslims being killed in Kosovo or to protect civilians from attacks by a tyrant in Libya? Cannot the accidental wounding or killing of even one 'innocent' civilian be justified by such humanitarian actions?

Of course, there are possible arguments about who is a civilian and what is innocence. But putting these questions to one side, we are still left with the problems of the 'just' war. Surely, any realistic morality must allow for policing of this sort? We must be able to exercise our duty to protect the weak from the ravages of the strong. Modern smart weapons are now so powerful and can be so precise that they can, errors avoided, reduce collateral civilian suffering to a minimum. That is surely the way to go.

Although painism tends to ignore intention as a morally important issue (in comparison with the actual *consequences* of an action) intention remains important when weapons of huge power are being employed. Killing or maiming a civilian intentionly is far less forgivable than killing or maiming a civilian by accident. The risks of such consequences must be taken into account. The British were absolutely right to abort an expensive RAF bombing mission on Libya in March 2011 when it transpired that civilians were near the target. Indeed, that episode marked a moral high point in the conduct of war in the twenty-first century.

What does painism contribute to the ethics of war? First it suggests that any warlike violence is wrong. Only if it meets all the requirements of a just war can it even be countenanced.

Secondly, however, painism allows the capture of delinquent war lords and dictators provided this is done on due authority (e.g. the United Nations) and without causing harm to others. Ideally there should be a trial of the target person in advance — in absentia, if necessary. At least a warrant for their arrest should be supplied in advance.

The taboo on the arrest or killing of dictators is not based upon ethics but upon the fear of heads of state that they all might become assassination targets. So this is not a moral argument so much as a political one. I would argue that taking out a criminal dictator is morally far preferable to causing suffering to a civilian or even to a military follower of the dictator. Far better, from the painist perspective is to focus upon the person responsible for the evil rather than on his ignorant or misinformed associates. Regime change is an ethical option.

Basically, we need an international police force — a United Nations police force — to effect the arrest of criminal dictators. If the criminal resists arrest then force, preferably disabling but even lethal force, can be used against them, provided:

- that all reasonable steps are taken to avoid harming others, and
- that the risk of harming others is low

As with any police force effecting the arrest of a violent criminal, proper care must be taken.

Tyranny by the Majority

Even a non-speciesist form of democracy has a further great difficulty and that is this: *democracy gives power to the majority over the minority.* So the wishes and welfare of individuals in minorities can very easily be trampled. Actually, a mere head count seems a most unsatisfactory way to decide any moral issue, not least because it ignores the feelings of the minority and, even more importantly, the *strengths* of their feelings. Take the case where ten people in an elected village council vote to build a road across another villager's garden because this would be mildly convenient for them. Only the affected person votes against the plan. So this is a vote of 10 to 1 in favour. It is clearly democratic to proceed with the road, although it is hard on the distraught minority voter. In this case ten people who feel mildly about an issue are overruling one who feels extremely strongly. So the mere convenience of ten outweighs the misery of one. Let us say that each of the ten voters in the majority feels 1 unit of pleasure at the decision: for a Utilitarian that gives a total of 10 units of pleasure in support of the vote. The garden owner, however, feels 7 units of pain and distress. In such a case Utilitarianism would agree with democracy (it often does so) by arguing that the decision is morally right because the total of 10 units of pleasure outweighs the 7 units of pain. Many of the political decisions in the Western world are taken upon this democratic principle and Utilitarianism is used to underpin it. The greater the majority the more likely it is considered to be that the grand total of pleasures (however slight they are in each individual case) will outweigh the pains of the minority. It can be seen that, in general, *democracy encourages the view that the mere convenience of a large number of citizens outweighs the agonies of the few.* Clearly, this tendency has unsettled rather a lot of people over the decades and, in order to reduce the number of worst cases, the courts have increasingly invoked the concept of human rights as a safeguard. So in the case of the garden owner, for example, a court (probably unelected) might well decide that, although the building of the road was indeed a democratic decision by 10 votes to 1, nevertheless the garden owner's property rights have been infringed and the decision is overruled. The individual is, rightly, regarded as sacrosanct. So rights are allowed to trump democracy.

I feel this is an unsatisfactory and clumsy way to run our lives. Democracy and Utilitarianism (both favouring majorities) argue one way while Rights Theory (supporting the individual) argues the opposite. It is a strangely stop-go or go-stop way to run a society. Cruel decisions are followed by stressful and expensive appeals and counter-appeals. Far better, surely, to look at every individual's pains and pleasures separately and to decide in favour of first reducing the pains of the maximum sufferers. In this way we can get it correct from the word go and not rely upon all the stresses of a prolonged multiple-stage legal procedure. Unrestrained, the legal process itself risks becoming a form of torture!

Conclusions

I believe painism, by ranking all so-called 'rights' into their varying degrees of pain- reduction (or pain-avoidance) effectiveness, provides a way to resolve any conflicts of rights. The solution is merely to give priority to whichever conflicting right is strongest in terms of pain-reduction. Ultimately, the only right is the right not to suffer unnecessarily. Painism also solves the problem of Utilitarianism's practice of adding up the pains and pleasures across individuals which can, as we have seen, lead to absurd justifications for painful experiments on humans, gang-rape and torture — and to democracy's similar problem of tyranny by the majority (see pp 75–80). Painism outlaws such totals while still permitting 'trade-offs' of pains and pleasures between individuals.

Perhaps painism's most obvious change, if it is adopted as a way of regulating our lives, will be that we no longer think in terms of measuring the badness of something by the *quantity of individuals harmed* by it, but by the *quantity of pain suffered* by those affected individuals (regardless of species) who suffer most. The quantity of individuals' pain matters far more than the quantity of sufferers. Yet it was claims about *the numbers of people* killed that justified the attack on Iraq in 2003 in the minds of at least some members of the British government[16] and 'the *sum total* of human hap-

---

[16] Jack Straw, BBC *Today* Programme, 4 March 2011

piness' was announced in 2011 as the basis for all new government policy in Britain.[17]

Suffering is everywhere — in every sigh and every groan, not just in moments of great anguish, grief and agony but in every tiny pang of guilt and shame, in every moment of frustration, in every little regret or ugliness or bitter thought, in every second of boredom or sadness, and in every wisp of fear or disappointment, every twinge, every itch, every fleeting niggle. Suffering happens a thousand times a day for each of us. Under most circumstances, causing or permitting suffering to unconsenting others is the one and only thing that is morally wrong.[18] So let us strive to reduce the sufferings of those around us, thereby increasing their happiness. Compassion is all. Believing in a morality can make us happier. So if the happiness of others is the aim of morality then morality is clearly a good thing!

Painism champions the individual — all individuals. Its aim is the reduction of every individual's pain and the enhancement of their happiness. This can be done through the universal application of known techniques to all painient creatures. More research into the causes of unhappiness and how it can be further reduced is required.[19] In education, rather than the laboured promotion of religions, a gentle enthusiasm for science needs to be taught, together with a greater emphasis on the discussion of benign and secular moralities.

Even with affluence, luxury, good relationships, work, health, freedom and a satisfying set of beliefs, much unhappiness will continue. How this residual unhappiness can be dealt with remains to be seen. Some of it will be in the form of clear 'clinical' depression and should be treated accordingly with medication and other appropriate therapies. The remaining residuum of (human) unhappiness may ultimately be reduced by participation in massive international

---

[17] Marie Woolf: Happy and You Know It? Make It Policy, *Sunday Times*, 13 March 2011

[18] Bertrand Russell: *The Conquest of Happiness*, Unwin, London, 1930

[19] *Five Ways to Well-being: The Evidence*, pub NEF 2010, and Margarette Driscoll: If You're Happy They Want to Know It, *Sunday Times*, 21 November 2010

campaigns that give a clear 'meaning to life'. I refer to huge communal projects such as the irrigation of the world's deserts, the exploration of space, dealing with climate changes and over-population, the understanding and spreading of happiness, the improvement of governance globally, and even with the eventual elimination of death itself.

Glossary

Algesic	Relating to pain.
Hedonic	Relating to pleasure.
Maximum Sufferer	The individual who suffers most.
Pain	Any form of suffering.
Painience (noun)	The capacity to experience pain or suffering.
Painient (adjective)	Able to experience pain or suffering.
Painism	The ethical theory advanced by Richard Ryder that defines the aim of moral action as the enhancement of the happiness of others, chiefly through the reduction of individual pain. Painism rejects the totalling of pains or pleasures across individuals, but accepts the calculation of cost-benefits between individuals.
Rights Theory	The ethical theory that defines moral action by according rights to humans or others.
Sentience (noun)	Being sentient.
Sentient (adjective)	Able to feel; capable of sensation
Speciesism	Discrimination on the basis of species. For the purposes of this book the author uses the term speciesism to describe human exploitation of and negative discrimination against members of other species.
Utilitarianism	The ethical theory that defines moral action as promoting the greatest happiness of the greatest number.

APPENDIX

Some Psychological Causes of Cruelty

For the purposes of this appendix I am defining 'cruelty' simply as 'the causing of pain or suffering other than for treatment or with the consent of the sufferer'. This applies to victims of all species. There are four main categories of cruelty and they are:

- cultural cruelty
- unintended cruelty
- instrumental cruelty
- deliberate cruelty

Cultural Cruelty

This includes not only such practices as bullfighting, dog fighting and shooting for sport but also any cruel treatments (such as female circumcision) that are accepted merely because they are customary. (The word 'culture' refers to the customs, attitudes and values of a society.) Most normal people in a culture unquestioningly accept its customs.

Customs also exist in smaller groups such as gangs, professions or religious groups. Such sub-cultures can include practices that are cruel (e.g. religious slaughter). The cult of machismo often provides a motive in cultures which encourage cruelty. Being cruel (and not allowing natural squeamishness or natural compassion to restrain such cruelty) is often, unfortunately, taken as a sign of manliness, especially in less developed societies.

Stanley Milgram's research in the 1960s demonstrated that some 60% of normal subjects will give apparently dangerous and painful electric shocks to unwilling subjects if authoritatively instructed to do so. (In fact, unknown to the subjects, the victims were actors and were unhurt.) Nazi and other organised atrocities can be understood in these terms. Ordinary people tend to obey orders and follow leaders.

Unintended Cruelty

This is where suffering can be caused accidentally, through lack of comprehension, poverty, psychological inadequacy or through illness, such as dementia or depression, in the perpetrator. Neglect is the commonest, but not the only, form of unintended cruelty. Often the perpetrator is unaware of the suffering he is causing, as in cases of pet-hoarding.

Instrumental Cruelty

Instrumental cruelty is where cruelty is caused as a means to a material end, such as in commerce, science and farming. In some parts of the world slavery continues and sex trafficking is widespread. As in some forms of fishing or hunting for food or fur, the cruelty is incidental e.g. in whaling or trapping. The perpetrator is often aware of the suffering caused but material motives (money), sheer habit, peer group pressure or respect for authority, dominate any opposing motivations such as compassion, squeamishness or moral repugnance. Perpetrators quickly habituate or get used to causing pain, so that they no longer feel natural horror or guilt at what they are doing.

Deliberate Cruelty

This is where cruelty itself is the main object, and it is usually carried out by individuals or by small groups following a leader. The basic motive is usually anger or revenge. Such anger is not always provoked by the victim. For example, the anger may be displaced from a human target onto an animal so that the victim becomes a 'scapegoat'. The animals get the blame.

Those suffering from conduct disorders, as well as sociopaths, frequently show violence (driven by anger) against both human and nonhuman animals. Their anger often takes the form of revenge for the perpetrator's real or imagined hurts already received (usually from humans). Sometimes violence can be a call for help or a means of obtaining attention. Children or animals are sometimes turned into victims or proxies for the perpetrator. Violence can be a feature of many psychological conditions (e.g. drug abuse, attention deficit disorder, conduct disorder, mania, borderline personality disorder, anti-social personality disorder or following head trauma). Often such violence is directed at animals or children. Such behaviours, especially if solitary, can also be a sign of incipient schizophrenia. Quite normal people, however, can also enjoy the sense of power and control that comes from cruelty.

Fear, too, can sometimes cause cruelty, and an individual afraid of attack may arm themselves and attack animals or humans before, so they believe, they themselves are attacked. Weapons include guns, knives and even animals (e.g. dangerous dogs) themselves. Sometimes such fear is delusional as in paranoid schizophrenia, or in other paranoid states.

The pleasures associated with sadism are essentially the pleasures of revenge and power. Sometimes, however, sadism can become associated with sexual pleasure. Some psychologists believe such sadistic potential is universal but is, in most cultures, unacceptable and thus contained. In war, when cultures are stressed, it may appear. A few cultures, e.g. the Roman and the Spanish, have traditionally valued some sadistic practices.

Cruelty to animals may be a way of showing off to, intimidating or hurting other humans such as the animal's owner. Serial murderers have frequently tortured animals early in their careers.

Children often see animals as 'people' or as members of their family just as humans are. The usual rivalries and jealousies can therefore apply, and so can the usual forms of bullying and meanness. Children need to be restrained in such cases. If parents or older siblings are cruel to animals then younger children may follow this example.

Conclusions

1) The causes of cruelty to animals do not differ substantially from the causes of cruelty to children. Some are associated with mental illness or disturbances in personality.

2) Over 60% of normal human beings will behave cruelly to people if they are authoritatively told to do so (Milgram) or if their companions do so. This helps to explain many of the Cultural and Instrumental forms of cruelty.

3) Being cruel to animals and being cruel to humans are often psychologically equivalent. The choice of animals rather than humans as victims is usually determined by the availability and vulnerability of animals and the reduced fear of detection and punishment.

4) Understanding the causes of cruelty may help find cures for it.

Curriculum Vitae

Richard Ryder read Experimental Psychology at Cambridge, researched in Social Psychology at Columbia, New York, qualified in Clinical Psychology in Edinburgh, trained in Psychotherapy at the Tavistock Clinic and worked as a psychologist in Oxford for twenty years. Later he took his PhD in Political and Social Sciences at Cambridge and became Mellon Professor in the Department of Philosophy at Tulane University in New Orleans. His books are:

Victims of Science: The Use of Animals in Research, Davis-Poynter, 1975; revised edition Centaur Press, 1983; Dutch translation, 1980, Norwegian, 1984, Hungarian, 1995, Russian, 1996

Animal Rights: A Symposium (Joint Editor), Centaur Press, 1979

Animal Revolution: Changing Attitudes Towards Speciesism, Basil Blackwell Ltd., 1989, revised version Berg, Oxford, 2000

The Political Animal : The Conquest of Speciesism, McFarland, 1998

Animal Welfare and the Environment (Editor) Duckworth, 1992

Painism : A Modern Morality, Opengate Press, 2001

The Calcrafts of Rempstone Hall : The Intriguing History of a Dorset Dynasty, Halsgrove, 2005

Putting Morality Back into Politics, Imprint Academic, 2006

Nelson, Hitler and Diana : Studies in Trauma and Celebrity, Imprint Academic, 2009

Biographical Note

Richard Ryder created the term *speciesism* while working in Oxford in early 1970.

As a key figure in the modern animal rights revival Ryder appeared on the first-ever televised discussion of animal rights (*The Lion's Share*, Scottish Television) in December 1970. Together with Bridget Brophy, Ryder then recorded several philosophical discussions for the *Open University*, again emphasising ideas around speciesism. He outlined speciesism in his contribution to the seminal philosophical work *Animals Men and Morals* edited by the Oxford philosophers Stanley and Roslind Godlovitch and John Harris in 1971.

From 1969 Ryder organised protests against animal experiments and bloodsports. He continued to promote his ideas about speciesism in leaflets and broadcasts in the early 1970s, culminating in the publication of his *Victims of Science* in 1975—a book that provoked debates in Parliament and on television and was described by *The Spectator* at the time as 'a morally and historically important book'.

Ryder declined Singer's invitation to be co-author of *Animal Liberation* (1975) because he was too busy campaigning for animal protection, but lent Singer material for this classic work. Dr Ryder was elected to the RSPCA Council in 1971, first becoming Chairman in 1977.

In 1980 he was founding Chairman of the Liberal Democrat Animal Protection Group, and later ran for Parliament, was Director of the Political Animal Lobby and then Mellon Professor in the Department of Philosophy at Tulane University. Ryder coined the term *painism* to describe his wider moral theory in 1990. He has several times broadcast on the BBC's *Moral Maze*.

Index

Abortion 116
Addison, Joseph 15
Ageism 121
Ahimsa 47
Anscombe, Elizabeth 34
Aquinas, Thomas 48, 114
Aristotle 3, 12, 14, 15, 31, 36, 48, 64
Asoka 46
Augustine 114
Austen, Jane 15

Banking 116 – 117
BBC 1,2
Bekoff, Marc 42
Benedict, Pope 122
Bentham, Jeremy iv, 13, 16, 32-34, 52, 56-58, 66-70, 72, 133
Blackburn, Simon 42
Bothamley, Jennifer 42
Bradby, F.H. 15
Brophy, Brigid 38
Buddhism 46, 63, 93, 97–100, 103
Bullying 118
Burney, Fanny 15
Buxton, Fowell 49

Castellio, Sebastian 65
Carruthers, Peter 55
Christianity 47, 48
Cicero 15,35
Commission and omission, acts of 87
Compassion 29-30, 68
Confucianism 63
Consciousness 39-40
Constantine 114
Copernicus 61
Cruelty 148-151

Daoism 63

Darwinism 1, 49, 50, 52, 72, 130-131, 136
Davidson, Richard 100
Dawkins, Marian 57
Dawkins, Richard 54, 67
Democracy 87, 119-120, 124-126, 128-129, 134-139, 142-144
Depression 102
Descartes, René 49
Divorce 118
Dryden, John 15
Duty to protect 139-142

Environmentalism 126-127
Equality 123
Edgeworth, Maria 15
Epicurus 94
Eudaimonia 14, 15
Euthanasia 117

Fairness 123
Faith Schools 127
Foot, Philippa 34
Foreign Affairs 127-129
Foundations of Morality 29-30
Francis of Assisi 48
Free will 8, 103-104
Freud, Sigmund 32, 94
Frey, R.G. 55

Gaddafi, President 141
Gillileo 61
Godlovitch, Roslind iv, 39, 57
Godlovitch, Stanley iv, 39, 57
Golden Rule 9, 10, 31, 47, 63, 67
Governance 134-139
Gray, Thomas 15
Grayling, A.C. 60-61
Gregory, Pope 23

Happiness 17-20, 23-29, 133
  as the aim of morality 12-14
  causes of 91-97, 100-103

Index

control of 97-98
correlates of 92-93
traditional views of 14-17
Harris, John 39, 57
Hedonia 14
Hegel, Georg 95
Hillel 10, 47, 63
Hitler, Adolf 11, 31, 35, 53
Horace 15
Houghton (Douglas) Lord v
Humanism 64
Hume, David 29, 68
Hutcheson, Francis 69
Huxley, Aldous 15

Ibsen, Henrik 15
Inland Revenue
 Commissioners 49
Inge, Denise 16
Islam 47, 63

Jainism 46-47, 63
Jamieson, Dale 62
Jefferson, Thomas 15
Jesus 10, 11, 47, 63, 113
Johnson, Samuel 15
Judaism 47
Just War 114-116

Kant, Immanuel 3, 12, 15, 20, 30-32, 36, 67, 68
Keller, Helen 16
Keshen, Richard iv

Layard, Richard 94, 96, 101, 102
Locke, John 29, 65

MacIntyre, Alasdair 34
Mahavira 46, 63
Maimonides 47
Martin, Richard 49
Marx, Groucho 16
Marx, Karl 64, 65, 95
Mautner, Thomas 42
McGinn, Colin v, 61
Media Ethics 104-108
Milgram, Stanley 4, 149, 151
Mill, John Stuart 16, 32-34, 49, 57, 69-70, 105, 112
Milton, John 65
Mood 23-29
Moseley, Michael 91
Morality as a component of religion 9-11
Moral Issues 104-132

Morris, Desmond 15, 54, 67
Moses 22
Murdoch, Iris 54, 67

National Anti-Vivisection
 Society 49
Nazism 11, 53
Negative Utilitarianism 84-85

Oswald, Andrew 102

Pain 17-20, 74-75
 grading of 80-82
Paine, Thomas 58, 65
Painism vi, 56, 59-60, 62-89, 72-74
 not adding across
 individuals 59-60, 70, 75-80, 144
 special provisos 77, 79-80
Paul, St. 48
Physical basis for morality 6-9
Pleasure 17-20, 74, 75
Police 126
Political Theory 119-121
Pope, Alexander 15
Portillo, Michael 137
Psychology of
 Pleasure/Pain 17-20
Psychology of Morality 3-6
Public interest 108
Punishment and crime 112-114

Regan, Tom v, 58, 59
Relativism 10-11
Religion 9-11, 20-23, 34-36, 46-49, 63-65, 90, 96-98, 103, 114-115, 121-123
Ricard, Matthieu 33, 99-100
Rights Theory 1, 3, 33-34, 36, 56, 58, 59, 65, 67, 70, 82-84, 87-89, 144
Rights 3, 65-67, 85
 measuring of 85-86
Royal Society for the Prevention of Cruelty to Animals (RSPCA) v, 45
Ryder, Richard iv-vi

Secular Moralities 64
Seven deadly sins, the 23
Sexual ethics 108-112
Sexism 121
Shaftesbury, Earl of 49
Shaw, George Bernard 15
Sikhism 63

Simms, Andrew 133
Singer, Peter iv-vi, 33, 40, 41, 57, 61, 67, 76, 79
Socrates 69, 88
Speciesism iv, v, 38-61, 89, 130-132
   attacks on 49-60
   definitions of 40-42
   leaflet (1970) 50-51
   lessons to be learned from 71-72
   manifestations of 44-46
Spencer, Diana 105
Stanford, Peter 17
Stewart, James 15

Ten Commandments, The 20-23
Torture 118-119
Tyranny by the majority 87, 142-144

United Nations 67, 85, 96, 116, 129, 139, 140, 142
Utilitarianism iv, v, 1, 3, 13, 32-34, 36, 56, 66-70, 75, 76, 78, 87-89, 133, 143
   its 'great flaw' 70, 75-80, 144

Victoria, Queen 49
Violence 124-126
Virtue Ethics 34-36, 64

War, just 114-116
Welfare State, the 118
Whately, Richard 15
Widdecombe, Ann 20
Wilberforce, William 49
Wright, Lord 49

Zoroastrianism 63